Why Christians are Skeptical of the Supernatural by Ernesto Aragon Copyright © 2018 by Ernesto Aragon All Rights Reserved.
ISBN: 978-0-9907697-4-3

Why Christians are Skeptical of the Supernatural

Ernesto Aragon

Published by: Ernesto Aragon

Seattle, Washington, USA

www.ernestoaragon.com

This book and parts thereof may not be reproduced in any form, stored in a retrieval system or transmitted in any form by any means (electronic, mechanical, photocopy, recording or otherwise) without prior written permission of the author, except as provided by United States of America copyright law.

All scripture quotations, unless otherwise indicated, are taken from the Holy Bible, New International

Version®, NIV®. Copyright ©1973, 1978, 1984, 2011 by Biblica, Inc.™ Used by permission of

Zondervan. All rights reserved worldwide. www.zondervan.com The "NIV" and "New

International Version" are trademarks registered in the United States Patent and Trademark Office by

Biblica, Inc.™

Scriptures marked KJV are from the Holy Bible King James Version

The names of the individuals used in this book are the actual names of the people unless otherwise noted. Some names have been changed to protect the privacy of the individuals.

First Printing: September 2018
Printed in the United States of America
Why Christians are Skeptical of the Supernatural

Endorsements

"First of all, I am very much thankful for my brother Ernesto Aragon who is the writer of 'Why Christians are Skeptical of the Supernatural.' I'd like to share that he explains very deeply the knowledge of Christ and his experience of getting together with other believers, and that's how our God works in our daily lives with His Holy Spirit. After reading this book, we will know how to change our lives for His Kingdom and also how our society affects our spiritual lives. I hope and believe that the readers of this book will be very blessed and gain the right knowledge and guidance that will lead to eternal life. I pray that God may give more power and blessing to this writer and his pen so that he may also preach about Jesus Christ, and this will be fruitful to all nations of this world, Amen."

Evangelist Sajad Shahzad
Founder/President of Gospel Mission Ministries Pakistan
https://gmmpk.weebly.com/

"One Encounter with God can change everything and Ernesto communicates this well through his own personal encounters along with biblical insight. The Kingdom of God is to be demonstrated not simply regurgitated. This book will encourage you to believe like Jesus.

There are too many Christians who ask, 'what would Jesus do,' when we need to be asking, 'what would Jesus believe.' Let this book ignite or reignite a passion for Him, people, the supernatural, and the limitless Kingdom of God."

Brian Orme
Founder of Kingdomstrate Senior Leader of Origins at UC San Diego
https://iborme.com

Acknowledgements

Mom and Dad — Thank you for always being there to keep me encouraged through the difficult times in my life. Without your help, I wouldn't be who I am today.

Jessica — You are an amazing sister and you've been such a powerful influence in my life!

Elizabeth Reisinger — If God hadn't strategically placed you in my life at the precise time He did, I wouldn't even be writing this book! Bless you my powerful obedient sister in Christ.

Eric Waterbury — You have showed me love in a way I have never seen before in church. Thank you for initially reaching out to me when no one else did. You are an amazing man of God and I want to follow Him through your giant footsteps!

Saul Lopez — You have been such a great mentor in my life! You've helped me many times to make better decisions in my life; thank you brother.

Naomi, Laura, Nicole, Andorful, & Eric Knopf — Thank you all for helping me to edit/revise and look over my book! You've helped me in great ways to be a more well-rounded individual through this journey.

Eugene Clark — Thank you for bugging me every so often about writing a book. You kept knocking and I finally opened that door!

Russell Breton — Thank you for challenging my mind to the point where I no longer desire to just write a book, but I want to positively transform people's lives and call them into their God given destiny!

Anyone else who I may have forgotten to mention, thank you!

Table of Contents

Prologue xi

Chapter One My Story 1

Chapter Two Your Background Matters 10

Chapter Three Biblical Theology and Divine Encounters 14

Chapter Four My Step into the Supernatural 23

Chapter Five Discerning False Signs and Wonders 42

Chapter Six The Gift of Prophecy 52

Chapter Seven Living the "Normal" Christian Life 64

Chapter Eight The World of Dreams 73

Chapter Nine The Signs and Wonders Movement 85

Chapter Ten The Spirit of False Humility 101

Chapter Eleven Walking in the Footsteps of Jesus 111

Chapter Twelve He Heals the Brokenhearted 121

Chapter Thirteen The Angelic Realm 133

Chapter Fourteen The Supernatural Power of Worship 139

Chapter Fifteen Comprehending the Mind of a Nonbeliever . 146

Prologue

The subject of the supernatural is a topic many Christians are uncomfortable with discussing. The definition of the supernatural according to the Merriam-Webster dictionary is, "Departing from what is usual or normal especially so as to appear to transcend the laws of nature." The great teachers, apostles, and prophets of the Bible such as the Apostle Paul, Moses, and John the Baptist most certainly believed in the supernatural power of God. If Moses didn't believe in the power of God when he reached the red sea, instead of saying "Thank you Lord," he would have said "Lord have mercy!" Most Christians don't have a problem believing that miracles happened in the Bible days, but the controversy revolves around the idea that they're still happening today. Generally, Christians today associate the supernatural with demonic forces. While it is true that not everything supernatural is of God, associating everything supernatural with the devil is like giving Popeye's spinach to a mouse. A lot of us are making the devil appear to be much bigger and stronger than he really is.

Jesus said in John 14:12, Very truly I tell you, whoever believes in me will do the works I have been doing, and they will do even greater things than these, because I am going to the Father. When He said this, some believe it was directed toward all mankind until Christ's return, but others believe that He was simply speaking to those living among Him while He walked the Earth. Can we still operate in the same supernatural power and authority God had given Moses, the Apostle Paul, and all His other disciples, or did those miraculous Gifts of the Holy Spirit cease at the perfect completion of the Bible as plenty of Christians believe is stated in 1 Corinthians 13:10? The revelation I am about to unveil will destroy the boundaries of human logic. Let us step outside the box.

Chapter One
My Story

Prequel

Before I was born, my mother had a prophetic dream about me. In the dream she was holding me as a baby in her arms while gazing into my grief-stricken eyes. As she was looking into my eyes, she could see that I was staring at something; it was a group of people dancing in a tree house. It was a setting similar to that of a night club. My mother was perplexed by my deep concern for the people in the tree house, because it's unusual for a baby to display such deep selfless emotion. I was seeing something that she was not seeing. Then, all of a sudden, there was an earthquake, and everyone fell from the tree and died. In the dream my mother realized that I wasn't crying because they were dancing, but because I knew ahead of time that they were going to die in the earthquake. This dream wasn't prophetic in that this specific event took place in reality, but it was prophetic in that the Lord had revealed I would be able to foresee events for the purpose of prayer and intercession.

My Background/Testimony

I was born in Oakland, California and raised in the Bay Area throughout most of my childhood years. I was/am blessed with two loving parents who have always diligently taught me the Bible. I accepted Christ at eight years old, and my life from that point on has never been the same. I was raised within the Protestant branch of Christianity, but until age twenty, I had never researched or asked many questions about my denomination. The general non-negotiables within Christianity that my childhood denomination indoctrinates are: The Bible is inspired by God, there is only one God but in three persons, Jesus was all man and all God at the same time, and Jesus will return on judgment day. I agree with all of these teachings as they're based on Scripture, but I am in disagreement with some of their teachings. With that being said, I love their churches as they're part of my roots. Today, I honor and support all Christian denominations that preach the message of God's love and salvation through Jesus Christ.

In saying that, I am the kind of person who is impossible to categorize denominationally. I do not consider myself to be part of any denomination or movement. I am a very open-minded person when it comes to learning about different Christian denominations, but I can be very firm in disagreeing with a teaching that is against the Word of God. While I am a firm believer in agreeing to disagree, there are denominations out there teaching that encountering God's tangible presence and experiencing His supernatural power is not for today; that is simply not true. As you continue reading, please allow the Holy Spirit to reveal to you His heart which surpasses denominational boundaries.

To my recollection, my first supernatural encounter with God was when I had a prophetic dream as a young child. The dream revealed that my sister was preparing to ask my brother and I if we wanted to watch the movie *Wild Wild West* starring the actor Will Smith. Sure enough only a few days after having the dream, my sister called and left a message asking my parents if she could spend the day with my brother and I at the movie theater; she wanted to watch the *Wild Wild West*. Since I knew nothing about prophecy, I dismissed the dream as just an unusual coincidence. This may have been my first divine encounter with Father God, but it definitely wasn't my last.

Growing up in the Bay Area from elementary school throughout high school, I would consider myself to have been a lukewarm Christian. I went to church every Sunday, read my Bible every night, and attended the local youth group services. I did all the things a good Christian boy was supposed to do. But in spite of all of these seemingly commendable activities, I was empty inside. I am not saying there is anything wrong with going to church every Sunday or reading the Bible every night, but if you're doing these things to be a good Christian, you will live a very empty life. In my adolescent years, emptiness and loneliness were two feelings I was all too familiar with. I was a very shy individual, especially at church. When it came to meeting new people, I always waited for the other person to introduce themself first. Once the other person would introduce themself, then I would open up and my real personality would be revealed. I had few friends, and with the few friends I did have, the conversations were very shallow.

I didn't understand the true meaning of being in a relationship with God. If someone had brought up the idea of being intimate with the Lord, I would have frowned at the thought. In high school, I had established somewhat healthy friendships within my home church, but it was more of a social club for me than it was a place to build my relationship with God. Toward the end of my junior year of high school, my family and I moved to Orlando, Florida which appeared to be the land of opportunities where housing was reasonably low priced. It seemed like a place where we could all start a new life.

In Orlando after graduating high school, I proceeded to attend a one-year technical school. I attended this school to satisfy my growing interest in cars and automotive technology. My favorite car at the time was a 1993 Mazda RX7 twin turbo. It was/is my dream car. This was the type of car every man wanted, but no one, who wasn't reasonably wealthy, could afford. I told my friends and acquaintances at the time that one day soon I would own that car, but I was told that my dream was unrealistic. One thing we need to remember as Christians is this: what's unrealistic down here isn't unrealistic up there.

 I started working overtime at my job to save the money required to buy the car. I was granted permission from management to work from fifty to seventy hours a week in several cases. After several months of working hard, I had finally saved seven thousand dollars. Since this type of car is very rare, it was highly unlikely to find one for sale in Orlando for a price I could afford. My family and I joined together in prayer on several occasions to find one close by, but nothing was found. I remember in one incident, I called a dealership to ask if this car was being sold at their location. The man on the other end of the phone stated, "Look, I know you really want that RX7, but everyone wants that car. That's a dream car, it's not realistic. However, I do have a nice V6 Mustang with a stylish body. Come on down and check it out, I think you'd like it." I was appalled by his suggestion as I knew exactly what I wanted, and he made a mockery of my desire. I told him "Thanks, but no thanks" with frustration hiding behind my calm voice.

 After all the months of research, I had finally found an RX7 for sale in Orlando from an internet ad. The car was everything I wanted, and more. The details in the car were exactly what I had secretly desired but never prayed for. The only problem was that it was ten thousand dollars and I only had seven thousand. I thought to myself, "If only I can quickly sell my current car for three thousand dollars, I will be able to buy that car." The car I had been driving at the time didn't have air conditioning. Selling it quickly for three thousand dollars in Florida where the temperature was consistently over ninety degrees all year round was highly unrealistic. But by faith, I put that car for sale on the same day I had seen the ad for the RX7. The next day, someone called about the car I had put for sale only the night prior. I informed the interested buyer that my car had no air conditioning and a small oil leak, just to make sure everything was understood. The interested buyer, knowing the car had no air conditioning, bought the car less than twenty-four hours after I had put up the "for sale" advertisement; it sold for exactly three thousand dollars.

With the extra three thousand dollars I had, I bought the RX7 only two days after seeing its ad. Though this desire I had was highly superficial, God still provided. God doesn't just care about the big things, but even our earthly desires like cars that will eventually rust and rot away [Matthew 6:19–21 and Matthew 6:33]. Through that experience with the car, God was getting ready to teach me a whole lot about my priorities in life and about where my heart truly was.

Eventually, my family and I moved back to California due to the housing market crash. We moved to a small town near Sacramento called Elk Grove. My relationship with God was very shallow after moving back from Florida, but at least it was there. My family and I began attending a small church in Elk Grove where we all started the process of rebuilding our individual relationships with the Lord. Things were going well; I even started getting connected with the youth group and developed new friendships. Everything was going well until the church announced that they were going to be postponing small groups for the young adults until further notice. The postponing went on for several months, until I ultimately lost contact with all of my friends. I continued to attend the youth service at the church on Wednesday nights sporadically, but everyone in the group was from high school, and I could not relate to any of the youth. At a certain point, I stopped attending the youth service altogether.

I would still show up at the Sunday services occasionally, but in the end, that ceased as well. I had finally gotten to a point where I didn't go to church at all anymore. The "good mornings" and "God bless you brothers" were all superficial talk, and no one really knew who I was. I became very depressed and started projecting my negative emotions on everyone around me at any chance I got. I eventually became suicidal, as living simply to work, pay bills, be a good Christian, and buy nice material possessions didn't seem worth it anymore; there had to be more to life. Over time, I began to drown out my sorrows with alcohol. I would drink so much that I would throw up and eventually black out. At this point I thought to myself, "Why would God want someone like me? I am definitely not worthy of Him. If I go to hell, then I certainly deserve it."

One day at work after several months of this had passed by, a young woman named Elizabeth Reisinger walked into the sales department of the tire shop. I said to her, "Hi, how I can help you today?" She began to explain to me the details of the issues with her car. While entering the information into the computer system, I decided to make small talk with her. Eventually I asked her if she was going to school and she answered, "Not yet, but I *will* be soon." When I asked which school she was preparing to attend, she said, "I am going to attend Bethel School of Supernatural Ministry." I was perplexed as I had never heard of a school like that before in my life. I responded, "Wow! What kind of school is that? What kind of things happen there?"

She answered, "Well I'm a Christian, and it's a school of prayer and divine healing. One of the things they teach is how to pray for the sick and see God heal people supernaturally." I thought to myself, "Could this be true? Are these things really still happening today? Is God still the same miraculous healer He was over two thousand years ago, and is it really happening at this school on a regular basis?" At a certain point, she invited me to her church in Sacramento. After this happened, I knew my life would never be the same again.

On a Thursday night, I had finally built up enough courage to visit her church. "She would be the only person I'd know, I don't think I can afford to make a thirty-five-minute drive every week," I thought, trying to talk myself out of it. When I arrived at her church, I noticed it was very large. I got lost in the parking lot and needed to ask a stranger for directions to find where the young adults gathering was being held. When I finally made it to the building, I walked inside, and my worst fear came true; she wasn't there. This meant I drove thirty-five minutes to attend a very large youth service where I knew no one. "I can't leave now, I might as well stay until the end of service to be polite," I thought. Despite my fears and to my surprise, the people were very welcoming. I enjoyed myself while making small talk with the men and women at the table where I was sitting. After the service was over I thought to myself, "This is a great church, a great service, and these are good people, but I won't ever come back here again."

As I started to make my way out the door, a man named Eric Waterbury stopped me and said, "Hey buddy, how are you doing?" Not really in the mood to chat and in a hurry to leave I answered nervously, "I'm good, I'm just visiting. I was invited by someone, I liked the service." Eric said, "That's good, who invited you?" I responded, "This woman, I forgot her name, um.... I think it was

Elizabeth or something I think." Eric replied, "Oh, Elizabeth! Yes, I know her very well, she is one of my spiritual daughters!" I replied, "Wow that's amazing, what a coincidence!" I had no idea what in the world a spiritual daughter was, but nonetheless, I was amazed by the circumstances.

Eric proceeded to give me his phone number and contact information, then invited me to his home for a Bible study and worship night. I thanked him, then left the church. Thoughts were racing through my head on the way home: "Who was that man? Does he really know her the way he says he does? Is this Bible study legit, or does this church organization have ulterior motives?" I wasn't used to someone being nice to me without wanting something in return; it was very unusual for me, yet I wanted to know more about this Bible study.

After fighting many difficult thoughts, I almost reluctantly went to the Bible study at Eric's home. When I arrived, Elizabeth, the woman who invited me to their church, was there. "At least I knew two people," I thought to myself. After my first visit to the Bible study, I immediately made good connections with the people from the group. I knew I would go back again. Years after attending the Bible study and church youth group, I got to know more people and developed many friendships. I started building a real relationship with Christ as the Bible talks about. I also started becoming more outgoing at church and began to introduce myself to newcomers to get to know them without ulterior motives. I took a class named Christ-Life which helped me to heal from my childhood hurts and pains, and now I am helping others with the knowledge of this Christian psychology course.

This same church youth group I attend today is very unique in that we believe in and experience God's supernatural power on a regular basis. I began to befriend people who were gifted in "word of knowledge" and prophecy. At a certain point, the spiritual gifts from my friends "rubbed off on me," and the Lord has been giving me visions, dreams, and words of knowledge for people not only attending my church, but also for strangers at coffee shops and non-believers alike. I've had divine healing encounters with God and have felt His manifest presence so thick that no feeling in this world can compare to it. While I will never be perfect in this world, I started stepping into my identity in Christ. The problem is that I'd noticed not every Christian was as excited about my experiences as I was. Christians I'd spoken with from other churches were telling me that my experiences with God were just my imagination. But was a divine healing encounter and a word of knowledge confirmed in great detail really my imagination?

Was I really so smart that I knew events would take place before they actually happened, and that I was able to guess names, dates, and detailed information about a total stranger and get it all right every time? Don't get me wrong, I'm pretty smart, but I'm not *that* smart. There is a God behind all of this who's providing information to me, and for religious reasons, many Christians questioned my encounters. There is a reason Christians are believing these lies and are stuck in traditional religion which is not Biblical. It's time for us to step into the truth and uncover these lies.

Chapter Two
Your Background Matters

History

According to the Center for the Study of Global Christianity [CSGC] and religionfacts.com, there are approximately forty-one thousand Christian denominations in the world today with the largest branches being Protestantism, Catholicism, and Eastern Orthodox. There is a misconception going around stating that these are three different religions; that is a false statement. Catholics, Protestants, and Eastern Orthodox belong to the same religion, but each believes and interprets the Bible in very different ways. The best way to visualize this for those who disagree, is to imagine a tree with three very large branches. With the tree being Christianity as a whole, one large branch represents Catholicism, another Protestantism, and the third Eastern Orthodox. Within each of these three large branches are many smaller branches with different beliefs inside of the same denomination. Is your head spinning yet? Good, mission accomplished. The purpose of this is to encourage us to research when our specific denomination was founded; this will better help us to understand why we believe the things we do.

A lot of us simply just believe what our parents and pastors taught us while growing up, but never aligned the teachings with the Bible. The separation within Christianity between different denominations is very similar to the telephone game most of us played as kids. All of us are sitting in a circular group whispering doctrine into the ear of the person to the right while the Bible is sitting in the center of the circle untouched. Some of the doctrine we are hearing is exactly aligned with Scripture, while other doctrine is a little off, but not a matter of debate. By the time that doctrine gets to those of us at the end of the circle, we are hearing things that are dangerous and actually contradict the Bible. Doctrine can change, but the Word of God has never changed. First and foremost, I want to say that I love all Christians; I am a Christian myself. As it says in First Corinthians chapter twelve, we are all the Body of Christ.

Although we are all one Body of Christ, a lot of us [like people in the telephone game] are hearing/believing lies about who God is and what He can do in our lives. One of many reasons Christians today don't believe in the supernatural is because of false doctrine they were taught growing up. There are typically three types of Christians: Some who believe miracles stopped at the completion of Scripture, those who feel that ninety-nine percent of today's miracles are false signs and wonders, and others who believe that miracles still happen today in the same measure that they did in the Bible. The problem is that not all of these beliefs are correct; there is only one truth. Either Jesus is the same yesterday, today, and forever [Hebrews 13:8], or He is not.

Religion

As I mentioned earlier, Christianity is a religion that is separated by countless denominations; yes, I did say Christianity is a religion. There is a popular saying going around stating that Christianity is a relationship with Christ and not a religion. While I am in one-hundred percent agreement with Christianity being a relationship with God, it is also a religion. In James 1:27 it says, *Religion that God our Father accepts as pure and faultless is this: to look after orphans and widows in their distress and to keep oneself from being polluted by the world.*

God doesn't hate religion; He hates the religious spirit. Religion is to Christians as a helper was to Adam [Genesis 2:18]. *Helper* is the title of a wife to her husband, not because that's all she is good for, but because the man wasn't designed to be self-sufficient in all aspects. *Helper* is the title that describes why God created a woman for Adam, but not the definition of what Adam was to pursue in Eve. In the same way, "religion" is the title that describes the co-laboring of believers with Christ as His helpers, but not the definition of what we are to pursue in Him. We are not to pursue religion, which would be like the title of being Christ's helpers. Rather, we should pursue what it means to be Christ's helpers; this definition of being His helpers involves relationship with Him.

Recognizing that we are pursuing a relationship with Christ and not a religion makes us passionate lovers of Jesus instead of religious people. The problem is that several Christian denominations are pursuing a religion and not a relationship with the Father. The Apostle Paul, prior to his conversion from Judaism to Christianity, was a religious Pharisee who had a beautiful relationship with his Bible, but not with God. One of the miraculous events that took place after Paul's conversion to Christianity [conversion from religion to relationship], is described in Acts 19:11-12 when Paul was so filled with the glory of the Lord, that even the handkerchiefs and aprons that had touched him were taken to the sick and they were healed.

The sad truth is that today there are Christians within many denominations that follow the same religious ideas about God that the Apostle Paul did prior to him finding Christ. Paul didn't know any better, as the Bible was incomplete when he got saved, but we do know better as now it is finished. By making that statement, I mean the Bible is finished, not God's power. Believing there is a God without supernatural evidence of His works is dead faith [James

2:17]. Jesus said in John 14:11 that if we don't believe He is God in the flesh by faith alone, at the very least, to believe Him for the miraculous works He is doing. Religion, also known as faith without works, is the reason so many Christians today are dead in the church. Religion is the reason so many atheists admit not going to church, because "it's boring." Going to church should be like driving a race car; if it's boring there's nothing wrong with the car, but there's something wrong with the environment providing the experience.

Chapter Three
Biblical Theology and Divine Encounters

A Boring Bible Study

During the winter of 2012, I began attending classes at a local community college. One day while heading to class, I saw a sign advertising a Christian Bible study. I was very interested, so I walked over to the group of individuals to talk with them and ask questions about their organization. I was very happy to see believers of Christ within the college environment. After breaking the ice, I began to share some of the miraculous testimonies happening within my own church setting and from Bethel Church: God healing people from knee injuries, paralysis, blindness, etc. After hearing this, the members of the Bible study looked at each other as though they had seen a ghost. There was a short awkward moment of silence which only lasted for a couple of seconds, but it seemed like an eternity. I felt as if I'd said something wrong, but I knew I didn't and became very confused by their reaction.

After the awkward silence, one of the members said to me, "We don't believe that humans have the ability to heal people. We believe that it is God alone that heals." I responded, "Yes I understand brother, and I believe the same. God uses us similar to the apostles and prophets of the Bible to pray for the sick, and by His power alone we are healed. Don't you believe that; isn't that what the Bible says?" One of the members seemingly bewildered by my question answered, "Yes, of course we believe that God can use you and I to pray for healing, as long as you don't believe that you're the one performing the healing." At this point I became even more confused, as I didn't understand why they appeared to be condemning me of being arrogant enough to say that I heal people. Within a matter of minutes, my simple testimony of sharing what God was doing in my church community turned into accusations of me being an arrogant fraud.

I responded to the members, "Of course I don't believe that I'm healing anyone, Christ is the one who heals, I am only His vessel." The two members looked at each other with an expression of uncertainty as they nodded their heads, appearing to only agree so that an argument wouldn't break out. One of the female members of the group overheard our conversation and walked over to us while smiling nervously. She said to me, "Yes of course we believe in those things, we will discuss all of these things in time. Here is a pamphlet to inform you about our study group. Are you interested in joining? You have already given us your email, so we will contact you and provide more details at a later date." As soon as we finished talking, I shook the hand of each group member, then walked away. As I walked to my car I thought, "That was just a simple misunderstanding; I'm glad we cleared it up!" But little did I know it wasn't a misunderstanding, but a huge red flag.

At the first Bible study, a small group of about five to six people showed up. The study wasn't anything deep, but it was simply explaining the foundation of Christianity: God is one in three persons, we are saved by His grace, and Jesus is the way to Heaven. I had already known all of these things but thought the Bible study was a nice way to interact with other believers in Christ. At the second Bible study I asked the group leader, whom I will name Sam, what their denominational background was. He said that they were not affiliated with any specific denomination. I thought to myself, "Okay, they must believe the same things I do."

At the end of the second meeting, I initiated a conversation with a lovely Catholic couple. I asked them general questions about their church and their hobbies. I later began sharing with them a non-biased scientific study from the University of Pennsylvania I had found on "Speaking in Tongues." The study mentions a segment of the brain known as *the frontal lobe* which is responsible for decision-making and thinking in general. In this study, scientists had been researching religious forms of meditation within different groups of people. These groups included Buddhist monks, Christians, and Franciscan nuns [Catholics].

In all of their research, it was discovered that the nuns and the monks had increased activity within the frontal lobe during meditation. On the other hand, when the Christians spoke in tongues, the frontal lobe had very little to no activity. For there to be no brain activity during the act of speaking makes no logical sense. This meant that instead of it being gibberish as many believe, there was something supernatural happening with the Christians that scientists could not explain. The young couple was amazed by what I was saying, and they were hungry for more knowledge of this phenomenon.

However, before I could finish answering the questions from the young couple, Sam [the group leader] abruptly cut me off by saying, "Ernesto I am sorry to inform you, but speaking in tongues is a spiritual gift that no longer exists today. Paul mentions in Corinthians that when the perfect comes, all spiritual gifts shall pass away. When Scripture was completed, there was no longer a need for spiritual gifts, as God's perfect Word had finally been finished. We are living in perfection, perfection is God's Word." I replied, "I don't agree with that, because I know a lot of people who speak in tongues." Sam smiled then responded, "Do you speak in tongues?" I answered, "No I don't, but I do have dreams from the Lord on a regular basis that come true." He replied, "But how do you know those are from the Lord and not your imagination?" I answered, "Well I know the devil can't be responsible for anything good coming to pass." Then he replied again by saying, "But how do you *really* know that is the Lord? You can't know for sure, because everything you hear needs to be in the Bible."

whether there be prophecies, they shall fail; whether there be tongues, they shall cease; whether there be knowledge, it shall vanish away. **For we know in part, and we prophesy in part. But when that which is perfect is come, then that which is in part shall be done away with.** This is one of the most controversial verses from the Bible debated by Christians today. Some Christians believe this verse to mean that perfection is the completion of Scripture [which is interpreted from the last two sentences in the Biblical passage above], while other Christians interpret this verse to mean that perfection is Christ returning for His Second Coming. Since there is only one truth, let us look into the Bible and tackle this misinterpretation head on.

In most cases, when reading the Bible, one cannot simply read a single verse and create a theology on it. Critical thinking [including studying the original Greek language] along with listening to the voice of the Holy Spirit must all be used when reading and applying Scripture to one's life. If we really want to understand what Paul was saying when he wrote that specific passage in Corinthians, we must read and break down all of chapter thirteen. Since I have already done this on my own time, I will simply provide the cliff notes here. In verses 1–3, Paul is speaking on the importance of charity/love.

Having love is above speaking in tongues, prophesying, faith, and performing good deeds for others. Verses 4–7 simply breakdown what love *should* be. Many people believe love hurts, but that's not in the Bible. Love doesn't hurt, people hurt. Now verses 8–12 are the most critical. In verse eight when Paul said *Love never fails*, he is letting us know that love will never pass away. Love is eternal when verses 4–7 are constantly put into practice.

In verses 8–10 [KJV], we know that Paul is saying that when the perfect comes, prophecy, tongues, and knowledge will all cease. Now the question we are all wondering is, what does *the perfect* actually mean? In verse eleven, Paul uses the analogy of a child's reasoning to begin his explanation of the perfect. A child's thoughts and speech are incomplete as he/she is still growing. But when a child grows up and becomes an adult, everything unknown becomes fully known. Verse twelve would be the best analogy of what the perfect means when Paul said, *For now we see through a glass, darkly;* **but then face to face:** *now I know in part; but then shall I know even as also I am known.* The words *face to face* are mentioned in both the King James Version and the New International Version of the Bible. Sure there are other translations where those exact words are not used, but the oldest and arguably the most accurate version of the English translation of the Bible is the King James Version.

Why is the specific excerpt *face to face* within verse twelve so important? It's important because Paul is describing the meaning of *the perfect*. If the perfect is described as seeing face to face, a reasonably intelligent person would safely assume that *the perfect* would have to be a person. Paul is saying that when we see a specific perfect person face to face, that is when the spiritual gifts along with knowledge will pass away. Since there is no perfect person in this world, the perfect would have to be Christ [1 Peter 1:19]. If the perfect is Jesus Christ, then the perfect has, in fact, not yet come. If the perfect hasn't come, then the Gifts of the Spirit along with knowledge are all for today until He returns.

When Jesus returns, speaking in tongues will cease because it will no longer be a language that is unknown; it will be fully known to all of us as our native heavenly language. There will be no prophesying when Christ returns. Since prophecy is designed to edify the Body of Christ and build faith as a sign for unbelievers, edification and signs will no longer be needed once perfection has come. Worldly knowledge will definitely pass away when Christ returns, because solving a mathematical equation or repairing a leaky radiator on your car will be the least of your concerns at that point.

Regarding the prophetic, why would Paul say in chapter thirteen that prophecy would cease at the completion of Scripture and then in chapter fourteen verse one, he tells us to eagerly desire the gift of prophecy? Either Paul has multiple personality disorder or he's just an evil hearted guy who takes pleasure in flaunting gifts we will never receive. If we believe that the supernatural gifts ceased at the completion of the Bible, then chapter thirteen and fourteen contradict each other.

A Divine Encounter with God

It is very important to understand that God cannot be put in a box. As much as I love knowledge and breaking things down, building and sustaining a love relationship with Jesus is something that is far too complex for the human mind to grasp. Contrary to popular belief, not *everything* God says is in the Bible. Everything God tells us will align with the Bible, but not everything we hear will be in it word for word. With that thought in mind, I will share what the Lord revealed to me several months later though a vision about this Bible study and its leader.

One cool early morning in September, I woke up in preparation to join friends in prayer for protection of the Christians being persecuted in the Middle East. While eating breakfast, the Holy Spirit reminded me of the members in the Bible study I had attended earlier in the year who didn't believe in the spiritual gifts. As the memories flooded back, I began to feel a deep burden from the Lord for the Catholic couple who was interested in knowing the truth, along with the other lovely individuals who wanted to know more. This thought almost brought tears to my eyes as I could see the spiritual hunger in them. They were tired of religion and were desperately seeking a passionate relationship with Jesus.

While thinking about these amazing individuals, I suddenly saw a picture of the group leader in a vision. In the vision, the group leader [Sam] was talking to the members within the Bible study. It felt as if my spirit was back at the Bible study, but my body was at home. Then I saw a picture of a little boy and for some reason I knew it was Sam's son. I heard very clearly that he was ten years old, and that he had dyslexia. At this point I felt as if everything I had been seeing was a dream, only I was very much awake and alert.

I figured the things I was seeing were just my crazy imagination. While I doubted it, I was still curious to find out why such a specific thought would pop into my mind out of the blue. I began asking the Holy Spirit to tell me what part of the human brain dyslexia is associated with. Before going any further, I just want to say that I, like most people, know close to nothing about the human brain. I closed my eyes while meditating on the Lord, then prayed that Jesus would reveal the name of the brain component to confirm that the vision was from Him. During prayer with my eyes closed, I began to see the letter "L." The name of the word was slightly fuzzy, and I couldn't pronounce it correctly. The name I thought I was hearing was *Lucordus Septum*. I decided to search on the internet for the name I was seeing to confirm that it was a real part of the human brain but found zero results. Since the name in the vision was fuzzy, I tried searching for different ways to spell the word just in case I wasn't spelling it correctly. After two or three tries, the web browser finally auto corrected my spelling and read, "Did you mean Lucidum Septum?"

I looked at the words in disbelief, then clicked the auto corrected link. As soon as the web page reloaded, chills ran up and down my spine as I saw several pictures of the human brain. I took a break from prayer to think about what was happening: "Was I hearing the voice of God?" By this point, it was almost impossible to disbelieve in what the Lord was revealing to me. But because of my analytical thought process, this wasn't enough confirmation. Sure, the Lucidum Septum [aka Septum Pellucidum] is part of the human brain, but I wasn't convinced that God was speaking to me unless that specific segment affected dyslexia directly. So, I decided to search on the internet again for, "Lucidum Septum dyslexia." After the results had finished loading on the web page, I clicked on two or three websites to read information about this subject. Every single website I visited confirmed that the Lucidum Septum is directly connected with dyslexia. After all of this, I needed no more confirmation.

I broke into tears and asked the Lord to forgive me for doubting Him and then got down on my knees and prayed for the little boy's healing. I didn't know that what I had received was a word of knowledge [1 Corinthians 12:8]. We can debate Scripture all day long, but no one can debate a testimony. *They triumphed over him by the blood of the Lamb and by the word of their testimony*

[Revelation 12:11a]. Some, after reading this, may believe that the power of prophetic revelation is of the devil. I would say to be careful with that mentality. In Matthew 12:24, the Pharisees thought Jesus was healing people with affiliation to "The Prince of Demons." Just like the Gifts of the Spirit have not yet passed away, neither have Pharisees; they just wear modern clothing and drive automobiles instead of chariots. Many Christians become skeptical when God does something that is beyond human comprehension. If we want to encounter God the same way Jesus' disciples did, we need to step outside of our minds and advance into His.

Chapter Four
My Step into the Supernatural

Preface: Supernatural Surgery

During another event that took place before I was born, my parents had an amazing encounter with God and His miraculous healing power. At that time, my mother had severe scoliosis which plagued her since birth. The scoliosis created a situation where one of her legs was shorter than the other. One day my parents heard that a healing evangelist was in town, and they decided to attend the service. By faith, they believed that God was going to heal my mother. During the service, both of my parents walked over to the evangelist to ask for prayer. Before my mother spoke to the evangelist, he [the evangelist] received a word of knowledge from the Lord and asked my mother if she had scoliosis. After answering yes, she sat down and lined both of her legs together. It was very clear that one leg was shorter than the other. The evangelist told my mother to close her eyes, but he told my father to leave his eyes open to watch what was going to happen. The evangelist commanded the shorter leg to grow out in Jesus name. My father, shocked and amazed, witnessed my mother's shorter leg slowly growing longer during prayer.

He witnessed the shorter leg grow out so far that it had started to grow longer than the other leg. The evangelist, with his eyes still closed, discerned that the leg was growing too far and commanded it to go backward into perfect alignment with the other leg. As soon as the Lord confirmed to the evangelist that both legs were the correct length, both my mother and the evangelist opened their eyes. My father had his jaw dropped, as he had never seen anything like that before in his life. My mother stood up to test out her back, and all the pain was gone for the first time in her life! The following day, my mother noticed that her back was very sore and felt as if someone had literally performed surgery on it.

There *was* in fact a surgery performed that day, and it was performed by the Lord Jesus Christ! The God who parted the Red Sea is the same God who heals today. I was born into a family that believes in the tangible power of God. Hearing about God's miracles that happened within my family that occurred prior to my birth was His way of priming my mind for His calling on my life. When a motor is started without lubrication, it self-destructs, but when it is lubricated prior to starting, it's prepared to handle the wild ride to come. In the same way, friction occurs between our minds and God when our previous ancestors never encountered Him tangibly, but when the supernatural runs in the family, our minds are primed for the ride the Lord is going to take us on.

My Introduction to Holy Spirit Encounters

The first time I ever truly experienced anything supernatural with God [prior to the Lord giving me the vision of the Lucidum Septum], was when I was at a small group Bible study. The guest speaker on this special occasion was a man named Brian Orme. I had heard many good things about this man regarding how powerfully God was using him in his ministry. After Brian had finished teaching at this Bible study, he had everyone line up and began praying for the needs of each person. During prayer, he laid hands on the foreheads of each individual while praying for the fire of the Holy Spirit to come. I watched attentively as people fell down during prayer. This was nothing new to me because I grew up in a Pentecostal type church, but I had never experienced that feeling myself. At that time, I was slightly skeptical of who was truly experiencing the power of God vs. who was putting on a show.

The moment Brian laid hands on my forehead I thought to myself, "I am not going to allow myself to look like a fool and fall on the floor like the others." As he began to pray for the fire of the Holy Spirit to come, I began to feel weak in the knees. Contrary to popular belief, he wasn't trying to push me down to the ground, but Brian had his hand positioned on my back to gently catch me should I start to fall. During prayer, I felt as if I was in a state of euphoria. I started to lose my balance and almost fell backward, but I stopped it because I didn't want to embarrass myself. I tried to continue standing, but eventually I ended up completely out of control and knelt down to the ground. This feeling was incomparable to anything I had ever experienced before. I have never taken drugs, but this must be what it would feel like. During this experience, I forgot where I was and felt as if I was floating outside of my body into another dimension.

At a certain point, I opened my eyes and everything happening around me seemed like a dream. What I had come to realize after this amazing encounter with God was that whether or not one believes in falling down in the Spirit [slain in the Spirit], it happens anyway. This experience was so real that even doubt and disbelief didn't stop it from happening. While the actual words "slain in the Spirit" are not mentioned in the Bible, there are many instances when the same experience took place. One Biblical reference to this is in Revelation 1:17 when John fell at Jesus' feet as though dead because of God's glory. Another reference is Revelation 5:14 when during intense worship, several church elders fell down under the

Holy Spirit's power and continued worshiping. Sadly, a lot of Christians who have never experienced this before are told this is the power of the devil. As Christians, we need to actually open the Bible and read it before we start saying things like that.

My First Experience at Bethel Church

Let's backtrack to January 2012. I [along with a group of friends] decided to visit a church known around the world for miracles, signs, and wonders occurring on a regular basis. A lot of Christians have heard of Bethel Church in Redding, California; it's the kind of church that you either hate or love, but it's difficult to feel neutral about it. Divine physical healing happens there often, along with supernatural manifestations of feathers, gemstones, and gold. It was a huge stretch of faith to believe that those things were actually happening. I was extremely skeptical and figured it was all fabricated and they just wanted to draw a lot of publicity. Despite all my doubts, the only way to know whether these things happening were true or false, I needed to experience it for myself.

When I first stepped into the church, my friends and I started walking around to explore different sections before the service started. Right away, I could tell this was a much different type of church then I had ever been to before. There were people praying for each other everywhere, and prophetic words were being given left and right. As I headed through the hallway, I walked past an older gentleman who was praying for a man. During prayer, the older gentleman touched my shoulder, and I felt an incredible power come over me that I'd never experienced before in my life. The power was so intense that I began to fall to the floor. Since I am not one to put on a show, I tried very hard to continue standing, but without realizing it, I was putting on an even bigger show by trying to resist the power of God as I squirmed around. It felt as if electricity was traveling through my body. After this experience, I felt as if I was high or drunk, only without negative euphoria.

A Spiritual High

I wish I could explain my encounter with better words, but that is the best way I can describe the feeling. A popular phrase today that describes this experience is, *drunk in the Spirit* [Ephesians 5:18-21]. For my description of this divine state of mind, I will simply call it a *spiritual high*. From my personal experience, the best way to describe this spiritual high is to imagine being drunk with alcohol. Before some of you start stoning me for blasphemy, I want to state the similarities and major differences between a spiritual high and actual drunkenness. With actual drunkenness, the alcohol slows the human ability to see, think, and make wise decisions. As a depressant, alcohol slurs speech and puts the body in a relaxed state of mind. Drunkenness [as most if not all of us probably already know] is usually accompanied by nausea, headaches, and vomiting. Alcohol eventually destroys the liver and brain cells when abused.

A spiritual high, on the other hand, puts the body in a relaxed euphoric state of mind similar to an *out of body experience*. Natural human senses are increased, and the ability to see and make wise decisions does not change. Fortunately, there are no negative side effects. During my spiritual high, I also felt a sense of completeness; having a high paying job, owning the perfect home with the white picket fence -- none of those things mattered anymore because my mind was set on things above. All of those things I mentioned are beautiful gifts from God that He blesses us with anyway, but when you are in a spiritual high, your only thoughts are on Him. In the midst of that state of mind, I felt complete and whole.

On the day of Pentecost in Acts Chapter Two, many people from different nations were filled with the Holy Spirit and started speaking in tongues. This spiritual high enabled people from different nations to all speak the same language at the same time; this defies human logic. This miraculous move of God was laughed at by religious people as verse thirteen says, *Some, however, made fun of them and said, "They have had too much wine."* The point I'm trying to get across is this... experiencing a spiritual high is of God and is mentioned in the Bible more than once. In the book of Ezekiel 3:23 Ezekiel says, *So I got up and went out to the plain. And the glory of the Lord was standing there, like the glory I had seen by the Kebar River, and I fell facedown.* Falling down in the Spirit and being overwhelmed by His glory is happening just as much today as it was in the Bible.

Bethel Morning Service

Since this church was very different than any church I'd ever been to, I listened to the pastor attentively to make sure the doctrine being taught aligned with the Bible. I had been to churches where a "feel good" Gospel was being preached, and part of me thought this was going to be one of those churches. Once I realized that the message of this church was very much Biblical, I let my guard down and allowed the Holy Spirit to work in my heart through the message of love and revival. Aside from the charismatic aspect of this community, I discerned the doctrine to be sound and rightfully convicting. During service, Pastor Bill Johnson received specific words of knowledge for people who needed healing. People were healed of knee injuries and chronic back pain in the middle of that service. Spontaneous healing also took place for people who didn't even receive prayer. By now I thought I had seen and experienced it all, but I hadn't seen nothin' yet.

Bethel Night Service: The Cloud of Glory

My first experience at the night service was one I will never forget. Night services are generally for worship, testimonies, and physical/emotional divine healing. Similar to most churches, the first segment of the service is worship. Initially, I noticed that everyone in this church seemed to be *very* passionate and engaged with the Lord during worship. I had never seen this type of excitement for the Lord within a church setting ever before; this excitement was contagious. After about fifteen to twenty minutes of worshiping the Lord, I noticed a single golden sparkle rain down from seemingly nowhere. I looked around and no one else seemed to notice it; I figured I was just seeing things. Then I started seeing more gold raining down. The best way for me to explain what it looked like is this: imagine seeing hundreds of gold shooting stars all at the same time.

I had heard about "The Glory Cloud" from my friends, but I was always skeptical. I figured it was either dust, or someone was dumping glitter from the air conditioning vents. The more we worshiped the Lord, the more gold rained down. At a certain point, it started to manifest as a cloud. Everyone started cheering and clapping, but I was still doubtful. Because I believed it was coming from the air conditioning vents, I decided to look straight up to a section of the roof that was far away from the vents. While gazing at the internal roof of the church, I saw gold manifesting out of thin air and raining down rapidly. After seeing that, I got butterflies in my stomach because I realized it was *real*. The glory of God started to fall during a song called "Our Father" sung by the Christian musician Jeremy Riddle. After about five minutes of this, I started to experience a spiritual high. After worship, everyone in the church sat down to listen to the message for the night. Throughout the message, I still noticed gold raining down lightly.

My spiritual high lasted throughout the entire preaching. I was very encouraged and empowered through the message by Kim Walker who is a powerful Christian musician and worldwide speaker. I was so filled with the Holy Spirit after the message was over that when everyone was asked to stand for prayer, I stood up and felt a weakness in my knees and almost fell down. I looked around just to make sure that no one had seen me [as it was embarrassing], but no one seems to give attention to things like that at Bethel being that it's so common. In sharing all of this, I'm not going to over emphasize testimonies on gold glory clouds, feathers, gem stones, or even gold teeth. While I do believe that God is certainly in all of these things and they are beautiful to experience, we shouldn't be flocking to church just to see these miracles. Going to church only to see signs and wonders causes us to worship the manifestations of God rather than God himself. I will go so far as to say that these manifestations can become idols to immature believers.

Where is all of this in the Bible? Concerning the glory cloud, in Exodus 16:10 it says, While Aaron was speaking to the whole Israelite community, they looked toward the desert, and there was the glory of the Lord appearing in the cloud. For supernatural feathers, Psalms 91:4a mentions, He [God] will cover you with his feathers, and under his wings you will find refuge. For gemstones, Exodus 24:9-10 says, Moses and Aaron, Nadab and Abihu, and the seventy elders of Israel went up and saw the God of Israel. Under his feet was something like a pavement made of lapis lazuli, as bright blue as the sky. As many may or may not know, lapis lazuli is a sapphire gemstone. Basically, Moses and the other elders walked on a pavement made of gemstones; that doesn't sound like something natural to me.

Nowhere in the Bible does God give people gold teeth to replace rotting teeth, but the Bible also doesn't mention anything about supernaturally replacing failed internal organs [I've seen it happen]. The point I'm trying to make is this: all of the miracles God performed could not possibly be recorded in the Bible. John 21:25 says, *Jesus did many other things as well. If every one of them were written down, I suppose that even the whole world would not have room for the books that would be written.* There comes a point in every believer's life when he/she must ask the Holy Spirit for answers to questions the Bible doesn't specifically mention. The answers will be revealed through the gift of spiritual discernment [I will touch on this later in the book]. I believe that God sends these visible signs to the world to simply build our faith in Him. As Bill Johnson always says, "These are signs that make you wonder."

Seeing Before Believing

As humans, we are wired to see before we believe. As Christians on the other hand, we are called to believe before seeing. Jesus said in John 20:29b, *blessed are those who have not seen and yet have believed.* Based on this verse, I feel that there is a greater blessing for those who have never seen God do anything supernatural, yet still believe. While it's true that there is a greater blessing for those who believe before seeing, Jesus also knows that there are those who need to see in order to believe. It grieves the Lord when He needs to physically manifest His glory for people to believe, but He does do it. In John chapter twenty, one of the twelve disciples [Thomas] didn't believe the others when they told him that Jesus had resurrected.

At the end of verse twenty-five Thomas says, Unless I see the nail marks in his hands and put my finger where the nails were, and put my hand into his side, I will not believe. Later in the week, Jesus walked through the wall of the disciple's home. He told Thomas to touch His hands and His side and said to stop doubting and believe.

Jesus wasn't pleased with the fact that He needed to manifest Himself to His disciples in order for them to believe, but He did it anyway because He loved them. Signs and wonders such as gold and gemstones only manifest so that we can build faith in the Lord.

In John 4:48 Jesus said [paraphrased], *Unless you people see signs and wonders, you will never believe.* While there will always be people that will never believe no matter how many signs are given [read the rich man's prayer in Luke 16:19-31], signs and wonders are ordained by God to transform the minds of people that have their hearts *open* to the supernatural. Signs are not only necessary to make the unbelievers wonder, but also the unbelieving believers. We are called "believers" not because we are skeptical of the supernatural but because we believe in it. To take this a bit further, Jesus said that signs and wonders will actually follow us if we believe Him! [Mark 16:14–20]

In saying all of this, I am *not* taking away from the fact that it is better to believe before seeing. In Mark 6:4–5, it says that Jesus could not perform any miracles in His hometown because of their unbelief. While it is better to have faith in the tangible power of God before seeing, God still manifests signs and wonders to *build* faith in those who do not yet believe. If we are going to church only to see signs and wonders, we are missing the point. On the other hand, if we are going to church to build a relationship with God and signs and wonders happen to be manifesting there, we are not to reject them. We need to come to a Scriptural understanding behind the purpose of these supernatural manifestations of God; when we come to that understanding, we can enjoy them while keeping our focus on Christ.

Casting Out Demons

One night, after having dinner with two friends of mine [whom I will name Devna and Samuel], we all decided to head to Devna's house to chat more and share testimonies. On the way to her home, Devna mentioned that she was troubled by demonic dreams. In her dreams she would laugh at the demons as if she wasn't afraid, but when she woke up she was terrified. The dreams would only occur when she slept in a specific room. When we arrived at her house, we were very quiet knowing there was demonic activity present. Before doing anything, I decided to gather all of us together in prayer to cast out the demon. This was the first time either of us had ever done anything like this. We all held hands and began to pray. After we finished praying, my right hand felt very weak as if a power had left me. Samuel was the friend holding my right hand during prayer. He had prayed with such power and authority, that I could feel the power of God being released into the room.

In Luke 8:46 Jesus said, *Someone touched me; I know that power has gone out from me*. The same power that came out of Jesus to heal the woman who touched Him is the same power I felt leave my right hand after we finished our prayer. After our prayer, Devna's demonic dreams did briefly continue, but something was different. In her new dreams, the demons were afraid of her because of the authority she had in Christ. The demons were saying to each other, "We can't kill her, she's too strong!" Demons are real, hell is real, and satan is real. Ignoring these dark spiritual beings leaves us prone to spiritual attacks but using our authority in Christ to cast them out makes them more afraid of us than we are of them [Luke 10:18-19].

The devil's Plan Revealed Through a Dream

One night while reading the book of Psalms, I became very passionate and expectant for the Lord to reveal something new to me, specifically through a dream. The verse I'd meditated on before bed was Psalms 34:19: *The righteous person will have many troubles, but the LORD delivers him from them all.* Sure enough, that night I had a dream. In my dream I was lying down relaxing when all of a sudden, I felt an invisible presence grab me from under my arms and lift me into the air. While in the air, I was extremely afraid as I could feel the invisible presence twisting and crushing my body. I realized that this spirit was satan. Then I remembered that I had power in Jesus' name. With authority I yelled, "Put me down **now** in Jesus name!" As soon as those words came out of my mouth, I was gently put down. But before I was able to recover from the experience, I felt invisible hands wrap around my throat. The pain from the chocking was unbearable and incredibly real. Somehow, I was able to cry out "Jesus" despite the pain, and the invisible hands slowly unwrapped themselves from my throat.

At this point all demonic activity stopped. Almost instantaneously, all pain related to the chocking and twisting/crushing discontinued. When I woke up, I felt no pain at all related to the dream. The Lord revealed to me that the devil was trying desperately to destroy me. In that dream, God gave me a temporary ability to see the evil forces attempting to come against me within the spirit world. Later the same day after having the dream, the verse Psalm 34:19 was heavily emphasized by a guest speaker at my church. I had never seen the man in my life, yet he was discussing the same topic the Lord spoke to me about earlier in the day. This was confirmation of what the Lord had revealed to me through the dream. The devil apparently wasn't/isn't very happy with me for stepping into my identity in Christ. The fact that the devil hates you tells you you're doing something right.

We cannot blindfold ourselves to the dark spiritual presence circulating throughout our world. A lot of Christians believe in the theology of hell and demons but refuse to believe in their spiritual attacks. Paul mentions in Ephesians 6:12, *For our struggle is not against flesh and blood, but against the rulers, against the authorities, against the powers of this dark world and against the spiritual forces of evil in the heavenly realms.* Imagine yourself blindfolded and walking into a four-way intersection without any guidance. Most of us would cringe at the thought of it. A lot of Christians are crossing the intersection blindfolded in fear and hoping to not get hit by the devil. The devil has a lot of power and authority when we're blind in the Spirit. God has given us spiritual eyes and ears that enable us to detect when he's coming.

Sometimes the devil takes pleasure in intimidating us by honking his horn while we're standing in the middle of an intersection as he races in our direction. Many Christians who ignore spiritual warfare run around like chickens with their heads cut off while the enemy is having a blast driving toward them at full speed. However, those believers who know who they are in Christ command the enemy to flee. As the enemy gets closer and realizes that you're not afraid, he swerves at the last minute in fear of hitting you. Satan has no power to do anything to you outside of God's will for you. Matthew 28:18 says, *Then Jesus came to them and said, "All authority in heaven and on earth has been given to me."* The truth is that for believers, satan has *no* authority.

Impartation for Word of Knowledge and Visions

While meeting for coffee with a good friend of mine, both of us began sharing testimonies of what the Lord was doing in our lives. My friend Laura is a very prophetic woman of God who hears the Lord's voice very clearly. Sometime during our conversation, I started sharing the prophetic dreams I'd been having on a regular basis that were all coming to pass. I was looking to her for guidance as supernatural revelation was new to me at that point in my life. During our conversation Laura said to me, "I believe it's not just gonna be dreams, but you're gonna start having visions." I smiled as I said to her, "That would be awesome, but that's not for me. I'm not able to hear from the Lord that way." Although I doubted what she said, I had no idea what happened at that moment in the spirit world.

A Vision

Prior to the events that took place in Chapter Three, I decided to attend a pre-service prayer at my church. Since this was my first time, I didn't know exactly what the procedure was. For this reason, I watched and listened to everyone else pray before I decided to say anything. As I closed my eyes, I started focusing on the Lord. After a short time, I saw a pure white horse with a horn sticking out of its head; I recognized it to be a unicorn. This unicorn was galloping across a very large empty field. Then all of a sudden, I saw the unicorn galloping toward a lot of black darkness. This frightened me, so I opened my eyes and realized that what I was getting was a vision. I couldn't believe what I was seeing while wide awake, but I asked the Lord for guidance as I closed my eyes again to see what was about to happen next.

As this unicorn continued galloping toward the black darkness, the image of the darkness became crystal clear; there were tens of thousands of black horses on defense ready to attack. When the white unicorn finally got close to the black horses, an extremely bright white light appeared behind the unicorn. If you can imagine, the light dispersed evenly along both sides of the white horse [unicorn]. The light was whiter than snow, like an angelic presence. Eventually everything behind the white horse was saturated with light. Then within a split second, the light wiped out every single black horse. After the defeat of the black horses, the environment surrounding the unicorn was pure white and a feeling of perfection engulfed the atmosphere. After seeing the vision, I shared it aloud with everyone. I had no idea what the meaning of the vision was, but I knew that light always overcomes darkness in the spirit world.

After sharing the vision, a man in the prayer group named Saul [my friend and a very prophetic man of God] confirmed that he saw the same white horse in his own vision. Later that night, I shared the vision with my father and he was shocked. My father said, "Did you know that the vision you had is in the Bible?" I replied, "Really?" as I was completely unaware of that at the time. My father then turned to Revelation 19:11-14 which says, *I saw heaven standing open and there before me was a white horse, whose rider is called Faithful and True. With justice he judges and wages war. His eyes are like blazing fire, and on his head are many crowns. He has a name written on him that no one knows but he himself. He is dressed in a robe dipped in blood, and his name is the Word of God. The armies of heaven were following him, riding on white horses and dressed in fine linen, white and clean.*

Then in Revelation 19:19-21, it continues, *Then I saw the beast and the kings of the earth and their armies gathered together to* wage war against the rider on the horse and his army. But the beast was captured, and with it the false prophet who had performed the signs on its behalf. With these signs he had deluded those who had received the mark of the beast and worshiped its image. The two of them were thrown alive into the fiery lake of burning sulfur. The rest were killed with the sword coming out of the mouth of the rider on the horse, and all the birds gorged themselves on their flesh. It's one thing to have a vision, but it's another thing to have it confirmed. Revelation becomes more real when there is confirmation.

Message of Knowledge

Several weeks after the vision of the white horse, I started noticing some very unusual things happening to me when I prayed for people. I started seeing images and began hearing inaudible voices. While at home praying one night, the Lord gave me a word of knowledge for my friend Laura. While listening to the Lord's voice, I began to feel confused for no apparent reason. I knew that wasn't my thought, and I discerned it as being an emotion from my friend. The Holy Spirit told me, *Laura is confused about something, and the answer will be revealed within the next week*. After sharing this with my friend, I waited for a few days to see what was going to happen. After seeing no results over a two to three-day period, I eventually forgot about it.

Toward the end of the week, I saw Laura in church and she said, "Hey Ernesto! So do you remember what you prophesied to me earlier this week? You said something about me being confused about something, and there's this apartment that I applied for a few months ago that I haven't yet heard back from. I know that it's not normal for an apartment application to take longer than a month, so I've been feeling frustrated and confused about that... but you won't believe what happened today; my application was finally approved!" It was amazing to both of us to see God moving powerfully through the message of knowledge [also known as a word of knowledge] He'd given me. 1 Corinthians 12:8 says, *To one there is given through the Spirit a message of wisdom, to another a message of knowledge by means of the same Spirit.*

There are a few stories from the Bible that talk about this particular gift, but there is one amazing story that stands out above them all. In John chapter four, Jesus sits down next to a well in Sychar Samaria to rest after a long journey. Jesus then asks a local Samaritan woman for a drink of water from the well. After talking to her for a while, He offers her living water which forever ends thirst. The curious woman asks Jesus for some of the water He is offering, but Jesus tells her to first go home and get her husband. In verses 17–19 the Samaritan woman said, *"I have no husband," she replied. Jesus said to her, "You are right when you say you have no husband. The fact is, you have had five husbands, and the man you now have is not your husband. What you have just said is quite true." "Sir," the woman said, "I can see that you are a prophet."*

At that moment, Jesus received a word of knowledge from the Holy Spirit. There is no natural way that He could have known about the woman's past and present situation without her telling Him first. Barron's marketing dictionary describes a message as, "The primary element of the communication process, consisting of the information passed from the communicator to the receiver." When God sends us messages, but we feel as though we're not receiving them, it's not because God didn't send us the messages, it's because we've ignored them. Because a word of knowledge is a divine message from God, Christians who are skeptical of the supernatural pay no attention to them. There are five natural human senses: Hearing, Sight, Taste,

Touch, and Smell. However, there is a sixth supernatural sense: Faith. How else is it possible to know that God will provide when our five senses are telling us otherwise? Skeptical Christians who start exercising their sixth sense will begin to receive and apply God's messages not only to their own lives, but also to the lives of others.

Healing

One night while worshiping the Lord at church, a friend named Sal received a word of knowledge. Sal walked up to the pulpit and said, "Earlier today, I started feeling a pain in my left ear. I immediately recognized this pain as not my own. Anyone who has pain in the left ear, please come to the front for prayer. The Lord is going to heal you tonight." After almost a minute of silence, two people stood up and went to the front for prayer. One person was an older woman in her fifties and the other person was a young man in his twenties. The young man had a consistent pain in his left ear. The older woman had permanent nerve damage on the left side of her neck leading to her ear. The pain from her nerve stemmed from a physical injury that occurred fifteen to twenty years prior.

First, Sal asked me to pray for the two individuals. We [Sal and I] commanded healing and complete restoration in the name of Jesus for the older woman. After only a few minutes of prayer, we asked the woman if there was still pain in her neck. The woman turned her head from side to side and started laughing as she said, "I haven't been able to do that in almost twenty years!" Afterward, Sal told me to declare healing for the young man's left ear. I commanded the pain to leave and reduce to zero in Jesus name and he was healed as well. Prior to this experience, I had never been used by the Lord to heal the sick. From this day on, my view of divine healing shifted;

healing was no longer just positive thinking, but a supernatural manifestation of God's love.

Visions, words of knowledge, and divine healing are all signs that make us wonder. Signs and wonders are used through the power of the Holy Spirit to increase our faith in Him and lead us to repentance. Stepping into the supernatural takes faith and is also the key to releasing God's power in our own lives. As amazing as it is to live a life of miracles, we need to be aware, however, that not all of it is of God. The devil is the master of deception. The enemy's goal is to take something good and create a counterfeit so that he can lead people away from God. One of our goals as believers is to unveil the devils blueprint so that we can destroy his works.

Chapter Five
Discerning False Signs and Wonders

Prequel

As Christians, we are not to give the devil too much credit by saying that everything bad that happens is from him. Sometimes bad things happen that have nothing to do with God nor the devil. If I'm driving 80 mph in a 65-mph zone and get a speeding ticket, I can't say, "The devil is always out to get me!" Sometimes we make bad choices that reap negative consequences. Now in that same situation, imagine being pulled over by the police and immediately being dragged out of your car. Picture the officer slamming you to the ground and giving you a brutal beat down without any explanation. This is obviously illegal, but these things do happen occasionally. Before the officer pulled you over, there was a subtle voice in his head telling him to beat you down.

The thought that crossed his mind wasn't his own but originated from demonic entities. Sure, what you did was wrong, but the punishment you received was far worse than you deserved. After a negative experience like that, you might develop a false mentality that says, "All police are corrupt." Without spiritual discernment, you will find yourself being transformed by your negative experiences rather than by the renewing of your mind [Ephesians 4:23]. Satan is the author of mind transformation through negative experiences. In Romans 12:2 it says, *Do not conform to the pattern of this world, but be transformed by the renewing of your mind. Then you will be able to test and approve what God's will is— his good, pleasing and perfect will.*

Most, if not all of us, would agree that there is a lot of corruption within law enforcement, but there is also a lot of protecting and serving. The devil's strategy is to corrupt one police officer, then shatter our trust to the point where we don't trust any of them. With a renewed mind of Christ, we forgive the officer for what he/she did to us whether that person has remorse or not. Forgiveness doesn't mean that we should avoid seeking justice for what happened to us, but it *does* mean that we're okay with whether it is served or not. Forgiving the officer disables the domino effect. When satan knocks down the first domino, his goal is to create a trickle-down effect which releases a blanket of hatred within our minds for them all. As the first domino hits the second within a renewed mind, the enemy discovers that the second domino is immovable. At this point, the devil's works have been defeated. It is important to understand that one man's flaw does not give us the right to condemn all men with the same authority.

The Definition of a False Prophet

In Matthew 24:10-11 Jesus said, At that time many will turn away from the faith and will betray and hate each other, and many false prophets will appear and deceive many people. There are two definitions of a false prophet. The first definition is: A person who falsely claims to have an ability to edify others through the foreseeing of future events, but contrarily utilizes the power of persuasion for self-promotion. The second definition is: A person given limited demonic authority to perform legitimate supernatural signs and wonders; the purpose of this authority is to slander the Gospel, and aid in the creation of a new world order.

Matthew 24:24 says, *For false messiahs and false prophets will appear and perform great signs and wonders to deceive, if possible, even the elect*. Knowing that there will be false prophets is important, because it is a warning for us to not be deceived into thinking that all signs and wonders are from God. False signs and wonders lead people away from God through the tactics of fear, manipulation, and control.

Before jumping into an example of a false prophet, I am going to explain what a false prophet is not. Jimmy Swaggart is a well-known televangelist who preaches the word of God in love and authority. As many people may or may not know, Swaggart was involved in a scandal over a decade ago which almost destroyed his life and his ministry. After living in darkness for a season, the Lord convicted him to come clean and confess his sin to the church and to the world. As a result, God blessed him tremendously and his ministry has flourished since. Many religious people however continue to judge and call him a false prophet even after his repentance. This is very disturbing to me, since our God is a forgiving God the last time I checked. While he certainly was in the wrong, we need to remember that "was" is the key word. Jesus said in John 8:7 [Paraphrased], *If any of you is without sin, let him throw the first stone.*

Jimmy Swaggart *is not* a false prophet. The only people who would call this man a fraud would be modern day Pharisees. We are no different than this amazing man of God, so judging him before taking the plank out of our own eyes is not very wise. God is not impressed by our sin, so we shouldn't be either. He knew every sin you would ever commit before you were even born [Jeremiah 1:5]. Many religious people have one bad experience in the church and never go back again because they expected perfection. In 2 Samuel, King David happened to notice a beautiful woman named *Bathsheba* bathing as he was gazing from his palace rooftop. He ordered the woman to come to him at once, and he slept with her. This eventually created a problem for King David because Bathsheba was a married woman. To solve that problem, King David started by getting Bathsheba's husband [Uriah] drunk one night. The next morning during Uriah's hangover, King David sent him to the forefront of a fierce battle where he was brutally killed.

Once Bathsheba's mourning period was over, King David married her. After the Lord severely punished King David for what he did, David genuinely repented. After all that, God still considered King David "A man after God's heart" [Acts 13:22]. If King David was still viewed as a great man of God even after committing that sin, we *must* forgive others for their wrong doings as well; there are **no** excuses. The act of forgiveness is so vital that Jesus said in Matthew 6:15, *But if you do not forgive others their sins, your Father will not forgive your sins*.

False Prophets and Counterfeit Signs and Wonders

Today there are new age Christian denominations and religions that combine the teachings of Jesus along with modernized thinking to redefine who they believe Jesus really is. The founders of these denominations/religions, due to their incorrect teachings, are false prophets. In many religions other than Christianity, Jesus is not viewed as God in the flesh, but simply as a mediator between God and man. Despite what the Bible says, these individuals don't accept that Jesus died on the cross and disagree with the idea of an actual Heaven or hell. There are many people who redefine who Jesus is, but the specific subject I'm going to discuss is divine healing. Some

Christian denominations, along with other religions, believe that God must always heal through prayer alone.

This dangerous mentality has led to many deaths, lawsuits, and suicides within these organizations. Aside from all of these sad stories, there are legitimate cases where divine healing happens. Mixing lies with partial truth however creates deceiving signs and wonders. By deceiving, I'm not saying that the miracles happening in these organizations are fabricated, but that the healing that does take place is not performed by God. The devil has limited ability to heal. In the religion of Santería, white magic spells are cast onto people who are sick, and the spells induce healing. I've noticed however, through my research on this, that when the devil does heal someone, something bad happens to the person who received the counterfeit healing. In the book of Revelation, Chapter Thirteen describes how the devil will give power to the anti-Christ in the last days. In that passage, we read about some of the limits of satan's power.

Verses 1–4 say, The dragon stood on the shore of the sea. And I saw a beast coming out of the sea. It had ten horns and seven heads, with ten crowns on its horns, and on each head a blasphemous name. The beast I saw resembled a leopard but had feet like those of a bear and a mouth like that of a lion. The dragon gave the beast his power and his throne and great authority. **One of the heads of the beast seemed to have had a fatal wound, but the fatal wound had been healed.** The whole world was filled with wonder and followed the beast. People worshiped the dragon because he had given authority to the beast, and they also worshiped the beast and asked, "Who is like the beast? Who can wage war against it?"

The Bible says that in the last days, the enemy will raise up one leader who will create a new world order. As of this writing, the new world leader has not taken authority yet, but we have already seen and will continue to see many anti-Christs. 1 John 2:18 says, *Dear children, this is the last hour; and as you have heard that the anti-Christ is coming, even now many anti-Christs have come. This is how we know it is the last hour.* It is important for us to discern which signs and wonders are of God, and which ones are not. In order to discern the spirit behind the signs and wonders, we first need to test them [1 John 4:1].

In order to test spirits to see whether or not they are of God, we need to know, according to Scripture, who God is and who He is not. For example, we know that God is love [1 John 4:8] and God would never contradict His Word [Isaiah 55:11]. Spirits that bring feelings of fear, anxiety, anger, jealousy, etc. are not of God because they contradict who God is. One of the most powerful quotes I've heard regarding the discerning of spirits is by Pastor Bill Johnson's grandson who was asked, "What if the Bethel Glory Cloud is not from God but from a deceiving spirit?" His grandson responded, "That's easy. If it's God, worship God. If it's not, worship God and it will leave." When you worship God alone, all deceiving spirits must flee so there's nothing to worry about!

There are many denominations where signs and wonders are taking place that are counterfeit. The best move we can make as followers of Christ is to love on these people because Jesus died for them too. I am not here to condemn anyone, rather my goal is to enlighten us with the knowledge of Christ through the power of His Word. As I mentioned earlier, it is not true that God must always heal through prayer alone. There are times when He chooses to heal by prayer, and other times He heals through the hands of a doctor. *On hearing this, Jesus said to them, "It is not the healthy who need a doctor, but the sick. I have not come to call the righteous, but sinners*

[Mark 2:17]." If you are sick and God isn't healing you through prayer, He wants you to go to the doctor! When Moses arrived at the Red Sea, he started praying to God that he and his people would be delivered. But Exodus 14:15 says, *Then the Lord said to Moses, "Why are you crying out to me? Tell the Israelites to move on."* There is a time to pray, but there is also a time to take action.

Understanding the Spirit World: The Power of Freewill

As believers [and even as atheists], most of us believe in the spirit world. A lot of us may not believe in God, but we sure believe in ghosts, haunted houses, and psychics; why is that? The reason is because in most churches, the supernatural is not something that is ever discussed because it is "too scary." In fact, the supernatural is discussed more on television shows, games, and in movies than in church. Because the supernatural is glorified so much from a secular perspective, most of us have the idea that God either isn't real, or He isn't very powerful if He does exist. Many people who call themselves *spiritists* don't believe in angelic or demonic deities [For more information on spiritism go to seratlanta.com and wikipedia.org]. Spiritists believe that the spirit world exists, but state that there is no connection between the spirit world and religion. People who follow spiritism believe in the idea of *neutral spirits*. I want to make something very clear regarding the spirit world; there is *no* such thing as neutral spirits. If we're communicating with the spirit world, we're either communicating with God, or unknowingly communicating with demons. The reason we have good spirits [Angels] and evil spirits [demons] is because they all have the ability to choose between good and evil.

In Genesis 1:27 it says, *So God created mankind in his own image, in the image of God he created them; male and female he created them.* God has given us a free will to choose between good and evil. If it's true that we're made in God's image, then God also has a free will. In the beginning when God created Adam and Eve, God created us to be like Him with a free will, but without a sin nature. When Eve decided to eat from the tree of knowledge of good and evil, the veil that covered sin was removed and from that point on, our natural ability to choose evil was born. A God that doesn't have a free will is a robot. God doesn't love us because He's programmed to, but because He wants to. Because "free will" is part of God's image, He created all living things with the ability to choose just as He does.

As in all of the living beings He created, spirits were also created with a free will. All spirits originated from Heaven, but one spirit [angel] named *Lucifer* wanted the Kingdom of God all to himself. Similar to humans from the beginning, no angel was created with a sin nature, but they *were* created to have a free will. In a metaphorical sense, Lucifer chose the tree of knowledge which created the sin nature in the spirit world. Lucifer said in Isaiah 14:13-14, *"I will ascend to the heavens; I will raise my throne above the stars of God; I will sit enthroned on the mount of assembly, on the utmost heights of Mount Zaphon. I will ascend above the tops of the clouds; I will make myself like the Most High."*

In order for Lucifer to satisfy his selfish desire, he tried to overthrow God from His throne. But because there's no sin allowed in Heaven, Lucifer, along with a third of the angels, was cast out of paradise forever. All spirits have a free will like humans to choose between good and evil. A spirit with a freewill can never be neutral. Just like spirits cannot be neutral, humans cannot be neutral. A person is either known for doing good or known for doing evil. There are people who some consider *neutral* because they're not really known for anything but staying out of trouble means you're a good person. Every spirit that roams the Earth was created by God. Whether that spirit chose to do good or evil after being created depends on the choice it made after the war broke out in Heaven. Communicating with spirits without using spiritual discernment is like inviting a stranger into your home; since you never know what you're going to get, *don't* do it.

From the time that Adam and Eve ate from the tree of knowledge, all of humanity had inherited the sin nature. The only person who was immune from inheriting the sin nature was Jesus. Because Jesus was not born naturally, He didn't inherit His mother's earthly DNA. Metaphorically speaking, Jesus had the free will throughout His life to choose between the tree of knowledge [which produced death] and the tree of life [which unlocked Heaven's door to eternity]. Because He chose the tree of life, He was and is able to provide the way to everlasting life. Just as Jesus had the ability to choose between good and evil while living on this Earth, spirits have a free will to do the same.

Let us not be deceived by the miracles occurring through the demonic practices of the occult. The devil's goal is to persuade us to follow him through a demonstration of his lying signs. The devil is one of the most beautiful angels God ever created and he will use that to his advantage. Christians have the authority though Christ to operate in God's supernatural power, and that is one of the most powerful tools we have been given to destroy satan's works. The devil is the master of deception and he will stop at nothing to intimidate us with his power. Nevertheless, the devil's power is limited because he is no longer connected to his power source. God has given us the ability to choose between Jesus, our true power source, and the devil, the disconnected king of lies. As Christians, we need to become aware of the infinite power and authority we have available to us through Christ. Once that realization takes place, the unplugged electric powered rifle the devil is using doesn't seem so scary anymore.

As I mentioned earlier in this chapter, the devil is going to rise up many false prophets in the last days and many people will be deceived. On the other hand, for there to be a false prophet there must be a true prophet. A lot of Christians are watching so carefully for false prophets that whenever a true prophet arises, he/she is spiritually stoned to death. As an example, it is important to meticulously check every one-hundred-dollar bill during a cash transaction because you want to avoid counterfeit bills. The way to determine whether the cash is legitimate or not, is by holding it up to "The Light." In the light, darkness has to flee, and the truth comes out. During many large cash transactions, you're bound to come across several counterfeit bills through the power of The Light.

On the contrary if you didn't have The Light, you would not be able to determine whether the bills are true or false. Many believers would rather throw out all of their one-hundred-dollar bills in fear that one of them may be false, than use the Holy Spirit's light to discern which ones are legitimate. As believers, it's time to turn "The Light" on and allow the Holy Spirit to reveal to us who His true messengers are.

Chapter Six
The Gift of Prophecy

Breaking Down the Gift

In 1 Corinthians Chapter Fourteen, the Apostle Paul tells us to eagerly desire the Gifts of the Spirit, especially prophecy. Prophecy is a sign for believers and also convicts us of sin. Out of all the Gifts of the Spirit, Paul considers prophecy to be the most important. Many of us may think that prophecy is a gift for ordained ministers, or for special individuals who pray ten hours a day and live in the mountains.

The truth, in contrast, is that prophecy is for everyone. Since we are living in the last days, the Spirit of prophecy is spreading like a wild-fire; Acts 2:17: *In the last days, God says, I will pour out my Spirit on all people. Your sons and daughters will prophesy, your young men will see visions, your old men will dream dreams.* The Bible says that all people will receive the outpouring of prophetic revelation, not just Christians. This supernatural revelation happening among unbelievers is leading many to Christ without the aid of any pastor or teacher. Prophecy is essential when spreading the Gospel of Christ. In fact, Revelation 19:10 [KJV] says, *And I fell at his feet to worship him. And he said unto me, See thou do it not: I am thy fellowservant, and of thy brethren that have the testimony of Jesus: worship God:* **for the testimony of Jesus is the spirit of prophecy**.

Prophecy is a gift freely given by God to those of us who eagerly desire it. On a side note, I want to say that prophecy is a gift and not an identity. Our identity is in Christ, not in the gift. By early 2012, I'd been having many prophetic visions and dreams on a regular basis. I was afraid of the revelation because I didn't know what to do with any of it. Many people think that it would be really cool to walk into a room like superman and know everything that everyone is thinking about. In reality, it's extremely burdensome if one doesn't know how to utilize the gift properly. After a while, I began talking to others within my church who also have prophetic gifts that could explain what was happening to me. Along with seeking the guidance of others more experienced than myself, I also dug deeper into the Scriptures. Something I learned through that growing season was that a person who prophesies is not necessarily any more spiritually mature than a person who doesn't.

Prophesying is solely motivated by love. Prophecy is designed to bring people closer together, to heal the sick, to reveal and prepare people for positive/negative future events, and to edify. A prophetic word not motivated by love is not of God, because God is love. Operating in the gift of prophecy without love is so dangerous that Jesus said in Matthew 7:21-23, *"Not everyone who says to me, 'Lord, Lord,' will enter the kingdom of heaven, but only the one who does the will of my Father who is in heaven. Many will say to me on that day, 'Lord, Lord, did we not prophesy in your name and in your name drive out demons and in your name perform many miracles?' Then I will tell them plainly, 'I never knew you. Away from me, you evildoers!'"* Love is who God is; we are God's vessels who transfer His love into others through the Spirit of prophecy.

While giving a prophetic word, it is important to understand that you can hear up to three different voices in your head at the same time: the voice of God, the voice of yourself, and the voice of the devil. Most of the time it's just God and yourself, but sometimes the devil likes to throw in confusion because that's just the kind of guy he is. After discerning which voice/spirit has given you the prophetic word, [I explained how to discern spirits in the previous chapter] if you have come to the conclusion that the voice/spirit was from God, then you must ask the Holy Spirit whether or not to share the prophetic word now. Sometimes the answer is *yes*, sometimes it's *no*, and other times it's *not yet*. Giving a premature prophetic word is not edifying, and in many cases, it causes division. There are times when God gives you a prophetic word that is never to be shared at all because it would never be received properly. During those times, He expects you to understand the other person's situation when most people probably wouldn't. Finally, there are many times that God says to tell the person right now. Most of the time the person receives the word properly and it is edifying as it should be.

Other times, the person does not initially receive the word properly, and he/she becomes either angry or frustrated with you. In those situations, you will wonder to yourself why God told you to share it right now if He knew that would happen. Then after only a short period of time the person will come back to you and say, "I'm so sorry that I got angry with you when you shared that word with me, but I now realize that I really needed to hear it at exactly the time that you told me. If you didn't tell me at the precise time you did, I would be in a lot of trouble right now." We cannot control other people's reactions, but we can listen to and act upon the voice of God whose timing is always perfect. Now that we have a better idea of how to use the gift of prophecy, it's time for us to see it in action.

Testimonies: Jesus Loves Muslims

After I came home from my first time at Bethel church, the Holy Spirit told me to research Islam. At first, I was confused by the voice and wasn't sure what to do with it [as my discernment at that time wasn't very good], but I started doing research. I watched many informative documentaries, spoke to Muslims, and even read through the entire Quran and the Hadith [after reading the Bible cover to cover of course], taking many notes along the way. The more I learned, the more my heart broke for the persecuted Christians living in Muslim communities. Then I heard the Holy Spirit telling me to minister to and teach them about Christ. Since I really didn't know how to do that, I ignored the voice. Many of us as children have heard our parents say, "Don't make me come down there!" after we've been told to do something we didn't feel like doing. After God told me to minister to Muslims, He decided to come down and encounter me in a way that changed my life forever.

From Debating to Obeying

One night while meeting with a good friend for coffee, we got into a very exciting subject regarding the supernatural. We shared testimonies of miracles, signs, and wonders that God was doing in both of our lives. A group of men sitting behind us became so interested in our conversation that one of the men interrupted and said, "I'm sorry to cut you off, but you guys are having a very interesting conversation over there. Would you mind if we joined you?" Neither my friend or I expected that, but I responded, "Sure, of course!" We began talking to these men about the miracles taking place in our church as they listened in amazement. At first, I thought they were Christians until they began talking about Ramadan and the Quran. By this point I'd quickly realized they were Muslims.

We talked with the Muslims for about three hours until the coffee shop finally closed down. We all had great respect for one another even though we had many disagreements. Out of curiosity, one of the men [whom I will name Andrew] asked my friend and I what type of Christians we were. I answered, "We consider ourselves nondenominational. We don't necessarily belong to any specific denomination or organization; we are simply followers of Christ." Toward the end of the night, Andrew and I decided to exchange phone numbers to keep in touch. After exchanging numbers, we both agreed to meet again. The only problem is that both of us had our own agendas pre-planned for the next time we would meet; I was trying to convert him to Christianity and he was trying to convert me to Islam.

When Andrew and I finally met up, we initially started talking about a lot of random subjects. After warming up, he began sharing with me how he had found the truth of Islam after converting from Christianity over a decade ago. Since I am a strong-willed person, I respectfully disagreed with him and shared Bible verses to back up everything I was saying. In defense, Andrew stated that the Bible had been corrupted and could not be trusted. We continued to debate for at least an hour and a half until we realized that neither of us were winning. After our meeting, I went home immediately trying to find more information to prove that I was right until the Holy Spirit convicted me. I'd learned that when sharing the Gospel, it's not about trying to convert anyone, but it's about presenting an opportunity. No human being has the ability to convert someone from another religion to their own because we each have our own free will.

We are not Christians because some wise salesperson with eloquent speech persuaded us to believe, but because we chose to believe. The only person who can convert you to another religion is yourself. Not even God will convert you; not that He *can't*, but He won't because it's against His nature. Since God is love and love is not self-seeking [1 Corinthians 13:5], He won't do it. After learning all of this, I decided to ask the Holy Spirit what He wanted me to say to

Andrew from His own heart. I needed to stop trying to be the wise and persuasive car salesman and start operating in my power and authority in Christ. 1 Corinthians 2:4-5 says, *My message and my preaching were not with wise and persuasive words, but with a demonstration of the Spirits power, so that your faith might not rest on human wisdom, but on God's power.* Jesus loves Muslims so much that He wants to demonstrate His love for them rather than just talk about it.

One night while in prayer for my friend, Jesus started speaking to me. He told me that Andrew enjoys studying Asian news and going to the beach. I saw many pictures of newspapers, the continent of Asia, and water/sand in my vision. At that time, I didn't know that the Middle East was in Asia, so it was difficult for me to understand why Andrew would be interested in Asia. In my final vision, I saw a picture of a hand and heard there was pain. After asking God which hand it was, He said, *"the right one."* Since I was very skeptical about the specifics of the final vision, I decided that I would only tell my friend about someone having pain in the hands whom God was going to heal. After Jesus finished speaking, I prepared a text message draft to send to my friend Andrew. Before pressing send, I asked the Holy Spirit if there was anything I had written in the message that wasn't from Him. He said, *"The only thing that is not of me is the fact that you didn't mention specifically the right hand."*

I was surprised by what I heard but decided to add *the right hand* to the message. The next morning Andrew texted me back and said, "I do enjoy going to the beach, that's true. I also hurt my hand about a week ago; the right one." After the confirmation, I prayed healing for my Muslim friend and thanked God for the revelation. Several weeks after this encounter, Andrew decided to add me as a friend on an online social network. After I accepted his online request, I saw a picture of a beach in his background which reminded me of when the Lord told me that he loves the beach. I also read that he graduated from Long Beach Community College. If we cannot be friends with people we disagree with, then we are preaching another gospel. Muslims are some of the most beautiful and unique individuals in this world, and one of the best ways to share the Gospel with them is by loving them through a prophetic demonstration of the Father's heart.

Love Came Down at Denny's

Late one evening, I decided to go out for a late-night dinner with a large group of friends from my church. After we finished eating, I exited the restaurant and waited for a few friends outside. While waiting, I noticed an African American gentleman probably in his mid-forties smoking a cigarette standing near the entrance. Then I heard the Holy Spirit telling me to talk to him. "How's it going?" I asked him. "Oh, I'm doing well young man, thank you for asking. How is your night going?" he replied. "My night is going great; this weather is amazing!" I said. Then the man started telling me that he was preparing for Ramadan.

Since I really wasn't in the mood to debate, I simply responded to his comment by saying, "Yes Ramadan, I've heard of it. I have a few Muslim friends who are preparing for that as well, that's awesome." After talking for a while, the man decided to ask me why I was meeting with so many people that night. I said, "Well I am part of a young adults' ministry at my church. We try to meet every week for fellowship with one another." Then the man said, "Oh I see, are you a Christian?" I responded, "Yes I am."

As soon as I responded, the man smiled as he said, "I used to be a Christian too, until I found the truth of Islam. I used to be Southern

Baptist when I was about your age, and I used to go to church and all that, until I started researching and found out that the Bible was corrupted. Did you know that?" By this point I was used to Muslims saying that, so I replied, "Yes, I've heard that before, but I don't just believe the Bible because that's what I was taught growing up, but because I experience it every day." I continued by saying, "Have you ever read verses in the Bible that talk about visions, dreams, and divine encounters with God? Well those didn't stop happening in the Bible, they still happen today."

"What do you mean?" he asked out of curiosity. I said, "I have seen friends of mine healed from physical injuries by the power of God simply because they had faith and trusted in His word. The Lord has also shown me visions and dreams that come to pass for the purpose of encouraging my friends and family. These things don't just happen to me, but to anyone who follows Jesus." After saying that, the man said something to me that I didn't expect. He said, "Can you pray for my wife?" On the outside I stayed calm and replied, "Sure no problem brother," but on the inside I said to myself, "WHAT?!?"

I had no idea at that time how to pray for a man of a different faith. "This man doesn't believe that Jesus is the Son of God, yet he is asking a Christian to pray for him?" I thought to myself. The man told me that his wife had some sort of life threatening cancer, and he believed that my faith in God would heal her. Since I am not one to procrastinate, I said to him, "Would you like me to pray for her right now?" He seemed surprised by my question, but he answered, "Yes of course!" In the Denny's parking lot, we both held hands and agreed in prayer for the destruction of the cancer in his wife's body. I prayed all of these things in the name of Jesus.

I was surprised that the man didn't stop me in the middle of the prayer and say, "Wait, I don't agree with that!" A lot of times when we are in difficult situations, we don't care if the person helping us is black, blue, red, or green. All we know is that someone has the ability to help us, and we need it. After the prayer, the man looked at me and smiled as he said, "Thank you brother, you're a real blessing." Then we hugged and eventually went our separate ways. I truly believe that it is important to study the culture and lifestyle of other religions for personal knowledge, but not for the purpose of debating. We should only be providing Biblical information to people who are asking questions. Doing this brings down the walls of defense, and the person becomes open to an actual heart to heart conversation. When your lifestyle demonstrates God's love, this act opens the door for the Spirit to flow.

Three Visions of a Boat

One day on a rainy Sunday afternoon, a few friends and I [along with my sister and nephew] decided to take a trip to Bethel Church. My friend Diana brought a Muslim friend with her whom I will name "Ahmad." Ahmad, at this point in his life, was very curious about Christianity and wanted to learn more. Once we made it to Redding, the weather cleared up just before the night service; we knew God was up to something good. As worship started, Ahmad gazed around the room not knowing what to expect. I closed my eyes and raised my hands as I began to worship the Lord. After maybe ten or fifteen minutes, I opened my eyes and noticed that Ahmad was gone.

I asked Diana where he went, and she said that she wasn't sure what happened to him either. I began to worry about him but continued worshiping the Lord. After worship was over, we all sat down in preparation for the sermon. My worry for Ahmad only grew stronger as no one knew where he was. Then finally about five minutes into the sermon, Ahmad came to sit down with us. He told us that during worship, someone he didn't know called him to the back of the church to share a prophetic word with him. The unknown person was of Middle Eastern descent and shared a vision with Ahmad. In the vision, Ahmad was being called to get into the boat of Jesus [to become a Christian]. Now I want to make this very clear, Ahmad told no one in the church that he was Muslim.

Ahmad went on to explain to us that two other unknown individuals from the Middle East prophesied over him as well; they prophesied *exactly* the same vision of the boat that the first person did. None of those individuals knew Ahmad and neither of them knew each other. Ahmad never had a supernatural encounter with God before, so he was a little afraid yet curious. After Ahmad told us that, and about forty minutes into the sermon, Pastor Bill Johnson said, "I feel like tonight Jesus wants some of us to get inside of His boat." Ahmad was very much overwhelmed that night, but he yearned to know more about Jesus.

It is important for all of us to understand that Jesus died on the cross for the entire world, not just for Christians. Jesus also died for Muslims and loves them the same as the rest of us. Most Muslims believe in the supernatural, but why don't Christians? I believe it is because of our culture. Most Christians living in North America are taught to believe that everything has a rational explanation. With that type of mentality, the Holy Spirit cannot operate. In the natural, a child who grows into an adult puts away childish things in place of physical and mental maturity. In the spiritual realm, a child who matures to adulthood only does so by traveling through the painful fires of this sinful world.

If that child makes it past the fiery worldly troubles, he/she has spiritually matured to adulthood. The childlike faith in the impossible remains the same after going through life's painful and negative experiences. The problem is that many children of God get stuck in the fire and can't see past their troubles. These "fires" of life keep many Christians in the infant stage throughout their lives. The belief in the supernatural slowly dissipates as feelings of worry and fear intensify. What we need to do is start kicking fear and worry out! This is the only way we will make it through the fire while maintaining our childlike faith in the insurmountable.

The reason I share all of these miracles is because He deserves the attention, and God wants to use you to do even greater works than these. God wants us, similar to the Apostle Paul and Jesus' disciple Peter, to demonstrate the power and authority we have through Christ to those who are searching for His heart. What you choose to believe about yourself becomes your reality whether it is the truth or not.

In order to live the "normal" Christian life as the great apostles and prophets of the Bible days, we must learn to develop a relationship with Jesus as they did. There is no formula to living a life of miracles, nor should we be seeking a formula to obtain that lifestyle. Loving Jesus creates an outpouring of spiritual gifts. Whether or not we seek the spiritual gifts has nothing to do with the level of depth in our relationship with God but seeking them does create a burning desire for more of Him.

The more we pursue Him, the deeper in love we fall. Falling deeply in love with Jesus erases analytical thinking, brokenness from past negative experiences, comparison, and disbelief. Without developing a genuine love relationship with Jesus, it is not possible to properly operate in the Gifts of the Spirit. In the next chapter, I will explain the importance of knowing the love of God prior to operating in His power. We are going to see what normal Christianity is supposed to look like.

Chapter Seven
Living the "Normal" Christian Life

Jesus is Our Example

It is normal to live the Christian life with an appetite for the impossible. The perfect example of what normal Christianity looks like is in the lifestyle of Jesus. Jesus did not perform miracles as God, but as man in the right relationship with God. Because of this we are able to mimic His supernatural lifestyle. Many Christians try to sell Christianity like it's a used car. We tell people about the benefits of accepting Christ, then share a generic testimony that even a non-believer could have experienced. While it is certainly wise to have knowledge of the Bible, it is wiser to demonstrate the power of God just as Jesus did. Demonstrating the power of God is not so people can be impressed with what He created, but so they can be impressed with the magnificence of their Creator. What's normal for Him should be normal for us.

Building a Relationship with Jesus

The most important point we need to remember is that everything Jesus did throughout His life was out of love. While signs and wonders *should* be normal for all Christians, the prerequisite to bringing Heaven's supernatural realm to Earth is learning to become intimate with God through a relationship with Him. In the Bible days, the Egyptians would spend their entire lives building pyramids. Many of the laborers never lived long enough to see the completion of the pyramids due to the amount of time it took to build them. In the same way, becoming like Christ is not a goal with an end result, but a life-long journey with an eternal destination. Developing a love relationship with God is the foundation of that pyramid. Some of the ways to build a foundation with Christ are by: reading the Bible, being in community with other believers, worshiping, writing, painting, etc. There is no order to how that foundation is built as long as a relationship with God comes out of it; God encounters everyone in a different way. The key factor in building that foundation however is by reading His word. Building a foundation in Christ based solely off of signs and wonders is like building a pyramid's foundation with feathers. Now most people can figure out why feathers would be a poor choice to use as a foundation for a pyramid. Feathers rarely stay still, and they tend to go with the flow of the wind.

Because the wind has such a great impact on the stability of a feather, it would be impossible to use it as a foundation. In Ephesians 4:14 [KJV] Paul says, *That we henceforth be no more children, tossed to and fro, and carried about with every wind of doctrine, by the sleight of men, and cunning craftiness, whereby they lie in wait to deceive.* Building a foundation on signs and wonders without knowing the love of God is not only foolish but dangerous. With a foundation of feathers, the pyramid tends to lean in the direction the wind blows creating great instability in the believers' walk.

The reason Christians who follow signs and wonders are unstable is because they have settled for being spectators of the supernatural rather than harvesters. As we learn to harvest the supernatural as Jesus did, we will cultivate a future generation of revivalists that will take our baton and do even greater things through Him than we did.

Identity

We are all sons and daughters of the King. We are all His children, but a lot of us don't know it yet. It is extremely important to know who you are as a son/daughter of God because when you do, it is easier to hear His voice and to operate in the gift He has given you. Without knowing who you are in Christ, you will gain no authority in your gift. There are some God-given gifts we have had since birth and there are other gifts we receive through impartation [Romans 1:11]. A lot of Christians who don't believe in the Gifts of the Spirit actually have God-given gifts themselves but are in denial. One of the reasons they're in denial is because they feel as if they're not good enough to deserve such a gift. To believe such a thing about ourselves is to say that what Jesus did on the cross wasn't enough.

Jesus died on the cross to cover all sins forever, even when we didn't deserve it. None of us deserve Heaven, and there is nothing anyone can do to earn it. If eternal life had to be earned, we would all be on the highway to hell. Because of all of the bad things I've done in my past, I would certainly be in the fast lane headed down south where the weather is always hot. However, because I am saved by His grace and not by my works, I am righteous regardless of my past failures or even my future mistakes. We don't receive any gift from God because we deserve it, but simply because we are His kids. We need to know who we are so that we can operate efficiently in our God-given talents.

The Effects of Sin Within the Christian Life

For a true follower of Christ, it is very difficult to sin, but not impossible [read Romans Chapter 6]. Sin doesn't separate us from

God because of grace, but it does create interference when it comes to hearing His voice. Imagine an antenna that is so massive that its height [from bottom to top] begins at the Earth's gravel and ends in outer space. Without sin, we are able to clearly hear from God and see Him moving in our lives. When we are living in sin however, it's like a dark cloud has passed over the antenna and it creates interference. In the midst of this darkness we are still connected with God and He is still speaking to us, but with the dark cloud of sin in our lives, we are not able to recognize God's voice as clearly as we normally do.

1 John 1:5-7 says, This is the message we have heard from him and declare to you: God is light; in him there is no darkness at all. If we claim to have fellowship with him and yet walk in the darkness, we lie and do not live out the truth. But if we walk in the light, as he is in the light, we have fellowship with one another, and the blood of Jesus, his Son, purifies us from all sin. While we're in the black cloud, the devil through his craftiness tries to convince us that Jesus is a liar; satan is the bowling ball who knows which pin to knock down first so that they all come crashing down. On the other hand, a believer living in righteousness sees the devil coming ahead of time and sends him to the gutter where he belongs. In saying all of this, sin is not something to worry about, but something to be aware of, especially while operating in your spiritual gift.

One night at my church during worship, I started to receive a vision from the Lord for a friend of mine sitting to my left. During this vision, I saw a video playing in my head of a nurse pushing someone lying down on a rolling bed into the emergency room. I heard voices echoing in my head that were not very clear, and then the vision started to become blurry as if I was losing reception. I tried hard to tune back in, but eventually I lost it. At that moment I realized that I lost the vision because my mind was plagued with fear and anxiety from something that happened earlier during the week. Because of the sin in my life, I was unable to hear clearly from the Lord. In the end, I didn't share the vision because I didn't fully understand it.

On another night at church during worship, I received a vision for a couple sitting behind me. The vision again wasn't very clear, so this time I decided to go to the alter to ask for prayer over myself. After I received prayer, the vision for the couple behind me became as clear as day. After sharing the word of knowledge with the couple, they confirmed that everything I said was accurate. I met with the couple for coffee a week later, and since then they have drawn closer together and even got married. It is essential to be free from sin while operating in your spiritual gift because you will either hear nothing and accomplish nothing, or you will deliver a message from the Lord for someone that will positively transform his/her life forever.

Love Never Fails

While the Apostle Paul commands us to eagerly desire the Gifts of the Spirit, he also says that without love, it all means nothing [1 Corinthians 13-14]. At my church we have a ministry outreach program we call *treasure hunts*. During a treasure hunt, a group of us head to the streets and give prophetic words from the Lord to strangers. During one of our treasure hunts, a small group of us decided to pray for a man sitting alone on a bench. One of the women from my group approached the man and sat next to him, as this is what the Lord told her to do. After only a short time, a conversation was initiated by the man. Once the man felt comfortable, a friend and I decided to approach the man as well. Immediately the man realized that we were Christians and he became defensive.

For a while the man vented about his life struggles and how God wasn't there for him. He explained how he had learned to accept his current life struggle as the Lord's mysterious will. Although we disagreed with everything he was saying, we nodded our heads as we listened to him vent; sometimes listening is all we need to do. As his venting eventually turned into ranting, I decided to give him a prophetic word. As I began to speak, he started to listen.

I started hearing the Lord say that he either enjoys traveling or wants to travel long distance someday. The man defensively told me that he doesn't believe in prophecy and everything I was saying was completely wrong. After I finished giving him his word, we asked him if he wanted any prayer before we left. He asked all of us first and foremost to pray for his daughter who was living in another country and he was worried about her safety and misses her a lot. Somehow the man didn't put two and two together but even in our disagreements, we simply loved on him. He let his guard down when he realized that we were not going to argue with him. At that point, he started to open up his heart not only to us, but also to God.

Love Brings Heaven to Earth

It is vital for us to understand that love is our stepping stone to operating in His supernatural realm. To understand how to love, I am first going to clear up some doctrinal errors. A lot of us may not understand exactly what I mean by "normal Christianity," so I am going to talk about what is abnormal so that we will better understand what is normal. It seems as if in today's society rather than Christians being transformed by the Word of God, the Word of God is being transformed by Christians. A lot Christians are being tossed around by the winds of doctrine and whenever something different comes along that sounds good, they all follow along. Now

I'm not saying that if I've never heard it before that it's wrong, but what I am saying is that there is new doctrine floating around that downright contradicts the Bible. Let's take a look at one of these false doctrines.

Turn or Burn

There are many Christians out there that try to scare non-believers into the Kingdom. I want to make something very clear before I go any further; the "turn or burn" theology does *not* work! While it is true that if a non-believer doesn't accept Christ, he/she won't inherit the Kingdom of God [Galatians 5:19-21], it is also true that if you don't replace bald tires on your car, it could roll over and the car could burst into flames. If a tire salesperson used that line on me as a customer and I knew nothing about cars, I would probably buy the tires out of fear but I would never go back there again. The message of truth becomes a lie when it is polluted with the counterfeit spirit of fear.

Since fear and manipulation are spirits that are not of God, using those methods to try and draw people into Heaven is actually demonic [2 Timothy 1:7 KJV]. When Scripture tells us to fear the Lord it doesn't mean we are to be afraid of God, but it means we are to have such utmost respect and reverence toward Him that disobedience is no longer an option [read Deuteronomy 10:12 and Deuteronomy 10:20-21]. Jesus is not in the business of scaring people into Heaven, but wants to love people into His Kingdom. John 3:16-17 says this perfectly, *For God so loved the world that he gave his one and only Son, that whoever believes in him shall not perish but have eternal life.* **For God did not send his Son into the world to condemn the word, but to save the world through him.**

Speaking Truth in Love

Instead, speaking the truth in love, we will grow to become in every respect the mature body of him who is the head, that is, Christ [Ephesians 4:15]. It seems a lot of Christians are either very good at speaking the truth without love or speaking a "feel good" message without any truth. As an example, we all know that the Bible says homosexuality is not okay, but many churches avoid the subject like a plague to stay away from negative publicity. Some churches promote homosexuality to gain popularity within the homosexual community; other churches, on the other hand, condemn homosexuals to hell before any of them get a chance to ask one question about Jesus. Both of these methods of reaching out to homosexuals are completely wrong. All we need to do as believers is love on the gay community and let God work on their hearts.

As I mentioned in an earlier chapter, God is not impressed by our sins, so we shouldn't be either. To God all sins are the same. God puts a liar in the same category as a murderer, and a child molester in the same category as a gossiper. While there are greater punishments on Earth for certain sins, God sees them all the same; they're all covered by the blood of Jesus. If Hitler repented and accepted Christ the day he died, he went to Heaven whether one likes it or not. The point I'm trying to make is that speaking the truth in love requires us to love and accept everyone equally without judgment of their actions. One of my favorite quotes by Pastor Kris Vallotton is, "Jesus loves and accepts all of us just the way we are, but He loves us too much to keep us the same."

Loving sinners doesn't mean scaring people to Jesus by telling them where they *don't* want to go, but it means to share with them what Jesus wants to do in their lives if they choose to follow Him. As John 3:17 says, Jesus didn't come to the world to condemn it, so why are we? I have plenty of non-believing friends of whom I am well acquainted with, and they all know I am a Christian because I'm a fairly outspoken person. I have not condemned any of my atheist friends to hell because that is not my job. When they want to know something about Jesus, they ask me. I don't ever volunteer information against their will. If we talk like Jesus but don't walk like Him, nobody is going to want to follow Him.

The Bible doesn't say, thou shalt be as a walking telemarketer going to and fro to condemn the world of their sin so they shall follow me or perish in the lake of fire forever, amen. Sharing the truth without love doesn't get us anywhere. Some of my favorite examples of Christ followers who preach the Gospel in love are: Bill Johnson, Kris Vallotton, Joyce Meyer, and Reinhard Bonnke. As we become perfected more each day in the love of God, we learn how to live the naturally supernatural Christian lifestyle with the same intentions Jesus did: to glorify God and lead the lost to repentance and salvation.

Once and a while, our heavenly Father gives us dreams to show us events that are either currently happening or haven't happened yet. Dreams are not only a normal part of the Christian life, but also a normal part of everyone's life. They're one way for God to demonstrate His love for us by revealing to us hidden truths about ourselves and/or others. Similar to puzzles, dreams are orchestrated in a way that every segment may not occur in an order that makes sense to the natural mind, but it makes sense to the Holy Spirit. I believe God does this on purpose so that we need to seek Him for the answers. I feel that dreams are one of the most intimate ways for God to love us through a visual taste of His supernatural reality.

Chapter Eight
The World of Dreams

The Bible and Dreams

Acts 2:17b says, *Your sons and daughters will prophesy, your young men will see visions, your old men will dream dreams.* To clear up some confusion in this verse, God is not saying that young men won't dream dreams and that old men won't see visions, but that all mankind will together experience this glorious outpouring of the Spirit in the last days. As an example of the importance of dreams, especially for non-believers, we will read from Genesis the story of Pharaoh's prophetic dream.

When two full years had passed, Pharaoh had a dream: He was standing by the Nile, when out of the river there came up seven cows, sleek and fat, and they grazed among the reeds. After them, seven other cows, ugly and gaunt, came up out of the Nile and stood beside those on the riverbank. And the cows that were ugly and gaunt ate up the seven sleek, fat cows. Then Pharaoh woke up. He fell asleep again and had a second dream: Seven heads of grain, healthy and good, were growing on a single stalk. After them, seven other heads of grain sprouted—thin and scorched by the east wind. The thin heads of grain swallowed up the seven healthy, full heads. Then Pharaoh woke up; it had been a dream [Genesis 41:1-7].

In this excerpt, we examine a clear example of God speaking to an unbeliever through a dream. The reason God was speaking to Pharaoh through the dream was because He wanted Pharaoh to seek Him through Joseph for the answers. God pursued Pharaoh through that dream with the intention of developing a relationship with him.

God wanted Pharaoh to seek His face for the answers so that Pharaoh would learn how to build trust in his heavenly Father during uncertain times. The fact that Pharaoh never did choose to follow the Lord is irrelevant to the story, but I share this side note because whether you choose to accept Christ or not, God never stops pursing you. As the rest of the story goes, Joseph interprets the dream to mean that there would first be seven years of great abundance, then afterward seven years of famine. Because Pharaoh believed in what God said through Joseph's dream interpretation, the people of Egypt stored food throughout the seven years of abundance and avoided what could have been one of the most disguisingly subtle, but catastrophic natural disasters since the beginning of mankind. God speaks to all of us through dreams whether we're Christians or not. Not all dreams have a profound meaning, [I will get into that later in this chapter] but for the ones that do, they simply mean that the Lord is calling us into our destiny with Him whether we realize it or not.

Another verse that talks about the importance of dreams is Matthew 2:13. This dream was extremely important considering it was about the safety of baby Jesus. During a dream in the night, an angel of the Lord appeared to Joseph and said, *"Get up, take the child and his mother and escape to Egypt. Stay there until I tell you, for Herod is going to search for the child to kill him."* After having the dream, Joseph obediently fled from Bethlehem with baby Jesus and his wife Mary. Once they departed from the city, Herod [just as the angel prophesied in the dream] ordered for all children age two and under to be killed in hopes that Jesus would be among them. However, as a direct result of Joseph's compliance to the Lord, Jesus' life was spared. If Joseph had been disobedient and dismissed the dream as a figment of his imagination, this world today would be a **much** different place to say the least. Yet because we know God doesn't make mistakes, He [God] chose Joseph knowing he was going to be an obedient and faithful servant. When God decides to speak to us in dreams whether they are warnings or promises, they come true regardless of our spiritual belief system or lack thereof. For this reason, it is essential to trust in the Lord when He speaks to us in our dreams, because only then do we become co-heirs with Christ rather than bystanders.

Bilocation

Bilocation according to the Merriam-Webster dictionary means, "The state of being or ability to be in two places at the same time." Bilocation in a physical sense is impossible because one being can never be in two different locations at the same time. In the spirit world, on the other hand, the natural laws of physics are void. It is entirely possible to be in two physical places at the same time while dreaming. While your body is asleep, your spirit can be in a completely different physical location witnessing events as they take place in reality. When it comes to Bilocation within dreams, one of my favorite verses that talks about it is Ephesians 2:6 which says, *And God raised us up with Christ and seated us with him in the heavenly realms in Christ Jesus.*

If our spirits are seated in heavenly places at the same time that we are living on Earth filled with the Holy Spirit, we are living every day in Bilocation. Based on Ephesians 2:6, I believe it is entirely possible for your inner spirit to stay inside of your body during a prophetic dream, while at the same time travel to another physical location to obtain information about a person, place, or thing in accordance to God's will. The outside information your spirit receives during your prophetic dream gets stored in your brain's memory compartment when your spirit returns to your body. Remembering your prophetic dream is only half of what God has called you to do.

Interpreting Dreams

Prophecy and dreams are intertwined in that they both involve hearing from God, the devil, and yourself. Because the two are intertwined, the same rules that apply for prophecy also apply for dream interpretation. 1 Corinthians 13:9 [KJV] says, **For we know in part and we prophesy in part**. *But when that which is perfect is come,* [Jesus] *then that which is in part shall be done away*. Because "The Perfect" has not yet returned, we continue to only prophesy in part. In the same way, we dream in part. Dreams, as I mentioned earlier, are similar to puzzles; God only provides to us part of the puzzle so that we need to seek Him for the perfect solution. During a dream, God will only reveal to us in part what He wants us to intercede in prayer for. Since there is a connection between prophecy and dreams, those who have the gift of prophecy already have the ability to interpret dreams. For those of us who are not prophetic, dream interpretation is a skill that can be learned by reading the Bible and listening to what the Holy Spirit is saying.

It is important during a dream to pay attention to your surroundings and to examine your feelings; are you located in a dark place or bright? Do you feel shameful and depressed, or excited and victorious? What type of symbols are in the dream? Symbols have a lot of meaning as they help us to piece together what God is trying to tell us. Some of the symbols within a dream are explained in the Bible while other symbols are specific to you and the Lord, and only you will know what they mean. Something also to remember is that every feeling in a dream whether good or bad *must* be aligned with the Word of God. As an example, one may feel a happiness and a freedom in a dream where they divorce their spouse and marry the person who's been flirting with them for years, but since divorce is not God's will, that would be a demonic dream masquerading as a revelation from the Lord.

In another example, you have a dream that you're extremely depressed and want to commit suicide. In the dream you see a rope and think about wrapping your neck around it to hang yourself, but for some reason you decide to look up and notice that the rope is leading to a hidden oasis. Then you begin to wonder if there really is another way to get away from your troubles other than suicide; you wonder if the rope could possibly be there to pull you to safety. Your hope was restored when you saw the hidden oasis, therefore your intentions changed. While a dream about suicide is not of God, a dream about hope is.

While I believe in God, I also believe in studying science. According to science, all dreams are inspired by the creativity of the mind. While I obviously don't agree that *all* dreams are based on the imagination, I do believe that some dream can be. Some dreams really do have absolutely no meaning whatsoever. There have been dreams I've had in which they appeared to have some profound meaning, but when I asked the Lord for an interpretation, He'd say, *"Son, that was just your imagination and it had nothing to do with me."* After hearing God say that, I'd laugh as I would think to myself, "I do have a crazy imagination, but that's how the Lord made me!" I'm happy to know that God does have a sense of humor.

Out of Body Experiences

There is a man by the name of Dean Braxton who died from a kidney infection for an hour and forty-five minutes. During that period of time, he said that he traveled to Heaven very quickly, but Jesus told him that it wasn't his time. Dean came back to life after almost two hours in Heaven to share his testimony with the world.

Out-of-body experiences [OBE] are very similar to dreams in that they occur during a state of unconsciousness, but for the select few who actually experience them, they state that OBE's are even more real than dreams. The human brain can survive up to six minutes after death and even longer if CPR and mechanical ventilation oxygenate its tissue. For this man to have been dead for an hour and forty-five minutes, the possibility of him dreaming is highly unlikely due to his experience taking place beyond the brain's six-minute window. What Dean experienced wasn't actually a dream, but a dreamlike reality of Heaven's perfection. People who have these experiences share how they can see the doctors operating on them trying to revive their own body; they're watching themselves in third person.

The Apostle Paul's Encounter

Although out of body experiences are not necessarily considered dreams, they're so similar in nature that some people have had this same experience within a dream. It is impossible to deny the reality of the spirit world as testimonies of these encounters arise. I believe the famous Apostle Paul had an out of body experience as he explains in 2 Corinthians 12:1-5. It says, *I must go on boasting. Although there is nothing to be gained, I will go on to visions and revelations from the Lord. I know a man in Christ who fourteen years ago was caught up to the third heaven.* **Whether it was in the body or out of the body I do not know—God knows. And I know that this man—whether in the body or apart from the body I do not know, but God knows—** *was caught up to paradise and heard inexpressible things, things that no one is permitted to tell. I will boast about a man like that, but I will not boast about myself, except about my weaknesses.*

To paraphrase, Paul explains in this verse that he knows a man fourteen years ago who was taken to the third Heaven [paradise], but he's not sure if he knows him through an out of body experience or not. I used the word (know) to refer to a past tense experience rather than (knew), because in the spirit world there is no such thing as (was) or (will), you only are. Read John 8:57-59 for more on this. I am first going to explain what he meant by the third Heaven. The first Heaven is also known as the sky. *And he prayed again* [Elijah], ***and the heaven gave rain,** and the earth brought forth her fruit* [James 5:18 KJV]. The second Heaven is known as outer space: *Immediately after the tribulation of those days shall the sun be darkened, and the moon shall not give her light,* ***and the stars shall fall from heaven,*** *and the powers of the heavens shall be shaken* [Matthew 24:29 KJV]. The third Heaven of course is the Kingdom of God: **Behold, the heaven and the heaven of heavens is the Lord's thy God,** *the earth also, with all that therein is* [Deuteronomy 10:14 KJV].

The reason we know that the third Heaven, according to Paul's description, is the final Heaven and house of the Lord, is because the Kingdom of God throughout the Bible is mentioned as **"The Heaven of heavens."** In the natural sense, imagine going to a car dealership and hearing the salesperson say, "Do you see this car here? This is **The Car** *of cars.*" In saying that, he in indicating that the car he is trying to sell you is the best of the best when it comes to cars; there is none greater. In the next excerpt of this verse, Paul explains his out of body experience. It appears to be that the Apostle Paul wasn't sure if he had an out of body experience or not, which is why he expressed his uncertainty by saying that he didn't know and only God knows.

Now what I'm going to share is not actually in the Bible, but it's more of a hypothetical scenario to get us to experience through words what Paul might have experienced in reality. Let's assume that in 2 Corinthians Chapter Twelve verses 2b-4, Paul is absolutely positive that he had an out of body experience. I find that by assuming he is sure of himself, it makes the verse much easier to comprehend. With that being said, if we only read the bold black text within the brackets, verses 2b-4 would say something similar to, whether **[It was]** in the body or **[out of the body]** I do not know—God knows. And **[I know that this man]**—whether in the body or apart from the body I do not know, but God knows— **[was caught up to paradise and heard inexpressible things, things that no one is permitted to tell.]** Since we know that Paul is referring to himself by reading verse 2a, I will replace the word "the" with "my" in verse 2b. Rephrasing this verse in simple English would read something like, **It was** [while] **out of** [my] **body, I know that this man was** [taken] **up to** [heaven] **and heard things** [impossible to be described through words], **things that no one is** [authorized] **to** [reveal].

Since everything I have written in the paragraph above is hypothetical, I don't want anyone to take what I have just spoken through my interpretation of Paul's encounter as Gospel. I am not trying to add or subtract anything from the Word of God, but I am simply formulating a hypothesis to teach us that we aren't the only ones who have unexplainable encounters with God; if Paul experienced the unexplainable, we can too. To my limited knowledge, the Apostle Paul could not interpret visions or dreams. This of course is purely speculation, but if we assume that statement is true, then there is no way Paul could have discerned whether or not he had an out of body experience which explains his uncertainty in the text. As I mentioned in chapter three, everything God tells us won't be in the Bible, but it *will* align with it. Out of body experiences are from God if they occur for us to intercede on His behalf for the safety or protection of someone else. According to my speculation, while the Apostle Paul could not interpret dreams or visions, Joseph could.

Had Joseph interpreted Paul's vision from 2 Corinthians, I personally don't believe there would have been any uncertainty expressed in Paul's text. Since we are the Body of Christ, we need to use all of the spiritual gifts the Lord gave us to do His work as one Body. We need to get together with other believers who have stewarded specific spiritual gifts better than we have so that we can mature in our knowledge of God. It was never His intention for us to mature spiritually on our own. Some of us are called to be Apostles like Paul, while others are called to be dream interpreters like Joseph. When we put our Pauls' and Josephs' together to do His will on Earth as it is in Heaven, we lead the lost sheep to salvation through the constant stewarding of not only our gifts, but most importantly our love [read Luke 15:3–7].

Out of Body Experience Reveals a Thief's Identity

My brother Lorenzo had been attending a church many years ago which had a men's home/shelter located on the second floor of the building. The purpose of the home was to provide a stepping stone for troubled men to get out of dangerous life-styles. The director of the home was not only a leader, but a living testimony to all of the men living within the men's home; he too had a troubled past which earned him prison time, but after accepting Christ he desired nothing more than to help others rebuild their lives as he did his. One day while the director was in the middle of a church service, he noticed a man standing in one of the pews who looked very familiar. As he took a closer look, he noticed that the familiar man was one of his former prison-mates. As the director's memories flashed back in time, he remembered this former inmate to be a devil worshiper. The director, remembering his former prison days, shared with Lorenzo that this former inmate was very deceitful.

After the service, the former inmate decided to have a talk with the pastor about joining the men's home. Since the former inmate knew that the director of the home was skeptical of his intentions, the deceitful inmate decided to attend a few church services to build his credibility. One night while my brother Lorenzo was asleep, he had a dream. In that dream, he felt his spiritual body float out of his physical body and travel to the church. As a spiritual being, Lorenzo witnessed a man breaking into the church during the night through a side door; he was identified as the devil worshiper. After the demonized former inmate pried open the side door, Lorenzo followed him into the church and watched the man walk downstairs into the pastor's room. First the man searched through the pastor's desk drawers, then later made his way toward the upper level of the church to the men's home. My brother witnessed the man walk into every room within the home. While the demonized man was searching through the men's home, he heard a noise. He looked back and noticed that someone was opening the front door of the men's home. Frightened, the demonized man escaped from the building through a side window.

After Lorenzo awoke from his dream the next morning, he decided to tell the men's home director about his out of body experience. When the director heard Lorenzo's dream, they both made a trip to the church to make sure everything was copacetic. Upon arrival, they noticed that the church side door had been pried open. When they went downstairs to check the pastor's office, his desk drawers were open with paperwork scattered everywhere; everything seen was exactly as the dream portrayed. Both the director and the pastor were surprised that Lorenzo was able to provide such intricate detail about the pastor's office and the men's home, considering he had never been to either of those rooms before. Ironically, after the church break-in, the demonized man was never seen at that church again.

John 10:10 says, *The thief comes only to steal and kill and destroy; I have come that they may have life, and have it to the full.* The devil is a thief, a murderer, and a liar who will find any way possible to destroy the Body of Christ. The devil's desire is to ruin the lives of people and remove their hope on Earth as it is in hell. As children of The Light, however, we know that light always surpasses darkness. The devil always makes his plans in secret, but when the Lord's revelation is provided through the dreams of His children, satan's plans are revealed. As soon as The Light enters any darkness within the Body [the church], that darkness has no other option but to flee the scene [Psalms 139:7-12]. When the devil forcefully enters your life and starts causing havoc, asking the Lord for His help pushes the door open just a crack to frighten the devil so that he jumps out the window of your life never to be seen or heard from again. Praying to the Lord for His help scares the devil away but knowing your identity and exercising your authority as a son/daughter of God keeps him away.

Visions and dreams can be very mystical, which is why a lot of religious minded Christians are opposed to believing that God can still speak through dreams today. Prophetic dreams are considered by many people to be associated with "The Signs and Wonders Movement." This movement is thought to be heretical for its teachings by many Biblical theologians. As I said before in Chapter Two, I don't consider myself to be part of any denomination or movement. I am simply a follower of Christ. From my research, I've realized that The Signs and Wonders Movement has actually helped many Americans today to believe in God's supernatural power. I'd like to provide information about the beginnings of The Signs and Wonders Movement while demonstrating to us why it is wiser to research a movement rather than to prejudge it. Many youths today cannot discern the difference between sound doctrine and New Age theology. Let's learn together how to analyze sound doctrine from the Word of God as well as apply it to our belief system without over analyzing the recent foundational history of miracles. Educating ourselves in the background of signs and wonders is important so that we know what we're talking about if people ask questions, but not to be focused on so much information that we over-think ourselves from believing in God's power. Let's learn through this next chapter how to become educated, level-headed supernatural warriors for His Kingdom.

Chapter Nine
The Signs and Wonders Movement

John Wimber

John Wimber is considered by many to be the greatest influence in the founding of The Signs and Wonders Movement. The movement began to emerge in the late 70's and early 80's but wasn't yet organized. Christians living in the US at that time who believed in the supernatural and experienced God's miracles regularly, generally didn't have a Body of Christ [a Church] where they gathered for spiritual growth. Most Christians in the United States during that time period were cessationists [belief that the supernatural Gifts of the Spirit had already ceased]. This same sad truth applies to today. Wimber wasn't born into a Christian family, but later in his life converted to Christianity.

John Wimber, as a new believer in Christ, was so hungry for God's Word, that he read and believed everything the Bible said. As a direct result of his faith, he experienced God's miraculous signs and wonders almost on a daily basis until he was taught cessationism. Wimber spent about twelve years of his Christian walk as a cessationist. During those twelve years, his supernatural encounters with God became less frequent because of his disbelief, but they still occurred from time to time. He was still very hungry for more of God during that time of his life but didn't know what he was hungry for; he felt disconnected but didn't know why. Later in his life, Wimber became a lecturer for the Fuller Church Growth Institute. Over time, he befriended a man named C. Peter Wagner who was a fellow professor at the institute. Because Wagner had been a missionary prior to becoming a professor, he had many testimonies to share with Wimber regarding God moving in Third World countries. Many of those testimonies included the sick being healed, demons being cast out, and other supernatural manifestations of God that made Wimber question his theological interpretation of the Bible. After this new revelation, Wimber later left the Institute and founded "The Vineyard Movement" which today has built over 1,500 churches worldwide.

In 1985 at a Vineyard conference, he said, "In my early experience in Christ, because I didn't have any of the kinds of emphasis that were standard of the church system in my background; you see one of the advantages of being a pagan before you come to Christ, is you don't have all of the negative baggage that goes with growing up in the church. And so, when I read the Bible, I just believed all of it. And as a young Christian I saw Jesus healing the sick, and so if somebody was sick we just prayed for them, they got well. And if the refrigerator didn't work, we just prayed for it too and it got well. And so did the car, and so did anything else we needed. And we were two or three years into that before we found out that God isn't doing that anymore."

No one is born believing that the Gifts of the Spirit have already ceased, that is something we need to be taught. As Christians, we wouldn't need to be taught that Jesus heals the sick because that's what the Bible says, but we *would* need to be taught that He doesn't. Cessationists believe that as we mature in Christ, God starts to make more sense. They believe that God is defined by everything that our five senses can perceive. In that belief system, God is limited to what our minds can comprehend. The reality is that as a believer matures in Christ through cessationism, that person matures out of a relationship with God into a religion. There is definitely a maturity, but it's in the wrong direction. Kris Vallotton, from Bethel Church, once said, "If you base your relationship with God on an experience you could be deceived, but if you read the Bible and never have an experience, you're already deceived."

Opposition: The History of Dispensationalism

Even though Dispensationalism has nothing to do with the formation of The Signs and Wonders Movement, it has a lot to do with the deformation of faith in the supernatural. For this reason, is it vital for us to understand where this way of thinking originated because it certainly wasn't the Bible. Dispensationalists [cessationists] are Christians that believe that all knowledge of God can only come directly from the Bible. They also believe that the Gifts of the Spirit are not for today. There were only three periods of time recorded in the Bible that miracles were consistent: During the time of Moses and Joshua, Elijah and Elisha, and Jesus and the Apostles [go to http://www.studylight.org/dic/bbd/view.cgi?n=531 to read more on this subject]. While cessationists believe that God does have the ability to perform miracles today, they don't agree that He would perform miracles in this generation the same way He did during those specific Biblical times. The reason this statement contradicts the Bible is because Scripture tells us that Jesus [God] is the same yesterday, today, and forever [Hebrews 13:8]. There are three verses in the book of Psalms that I have connected together to explain why signs and wonders didn't happen consistently throughout the Bible. Chapter 78:4 says, *We will not hide them from their descendants;* **we will tell the next generation the praise worthy deeds of the Lord, his** *power, and the wonders he has done.* Then verse eleven says, ***They forgot what he had done, the wonders he had shown them.*** Lastly, verse thirty-two reads, *In spite of all this, they kept on sinning;* ***in spite of his wonders, they did not believe.***

The reason miracles didn't happen consistently throughout the Bible is the same reason Jesus could not perform miracles in His home town; disbelief. God probably didn't perform miracles outside of those three periods of time recorded in the Bible because the people didn't believe. The reason I say *probably* is because not every miracle that took place in those days could have been recorded in the Bible as John 21:25 says. In contrast, God could have performed many more signs and wonders in those days that were never recorded. I say all of this because as believers today, we need to continue operating in the Gifts of the Spirit by spreading the word of His miracles to the generations to come. If we don't, we will end up with a world full of unbelieving Christians who are satisfied with knowing about a God who is powerful in theory, but powerless in reality. Just as I have explained the foundation of The Signs and Wonders Movement, I will also explain the background of cessationist theology. Though many conservative Christians may deny it, one of the biggest reasons for cessationism spreading within Christianity is because of "The Age of Enlightenment."

Why Christians are Skeptical of the Supernatural

The Age of Enlightenment [The Age of Reason] was a philosophy that was introduced into the United States back in the 1700's by many highly influential leaders. The purpose of this philosophy was to modernize the thought process of U.S. citizens by removing superstitious elements such as the supernatural. Because of this reformation, every religion in the U.S. was required to modify their belief system in order to adhere to the new movement standards. The Enlightenment movement not only transformed the minds of religious people, but all Americans. This is one of the major reasons Christians living in America are skeptical of the supernatural. Conservative Christians have always been skeptical even prior to The Age of Reason, but on a much smaller scale due to their lack of an organized anti-supernatural movement. Though The Age of Enlightenment ended in the 18th century, the idea of using reason over having faith continues to live on today. I'm sure there are many other reasons why Christians are skeptical of the supernatural, but this one takes the lead.

The Age of Enlightenment produced many modern-day Pharisees during that time era, and they have passed the baton to the Pharisees of the next generation; this needs to come to a stop. As I explained earlier in this chapter through Kris Vallotton's quote, "If you base your relationship with God on an experience you could be deceived, but if you read the Bible and never have an experience, you're already deceived," the Bible was never meant to be read without having a supernatural experience. We become deceived when we reduce healing to happen only through natural means, limit the gift of tongues to mean learning a new language, and understand the gift of prophecy to mean Bible prophecy only. If psychics and witch doctors believe in, and operate in counterfeit signs and wonders today, they're already more powerful than the average Christian.

If they're operating in the supernatural through counterfeit power, how much more effective would we be as believers if we operate in the supernatural through The Creator of all power? Just like cessationism has always been around even prior to The Enlightenment Movement, miracles have always been around even before the foundation of The Signs and Wonders Movement. Heaven has always been open; The Signs and Wonders Movement simply helped many Christians living in America to finally figure that out. In conclusion to the history of dispensation, I want to say that I am not against cessationist Christians; I'm against cessationist thinking.

Kingdom Theology

Kingdom Theology, associated with the Vineyard movement, teaches that the Kingdom of God exists in the world today, but only in part. The Kingdom of God becomes one with the Earth when His Heavenly signs and wonders become our reality. When the perfect [Christ] returns, is when the Kingdom of God will be fully known. Kingdom Theology teaches that the purpose of all believers is to bring God's Kingdom to Earth as it is in Heaven through signs and wonders. This comes from a few verses. In Mark 6:12, Jesus along with His twelve disciples went out preaching with love that people should repent. Verse thirteen says, *They drove out many demons and anointed many sick people with oil and healed them*. In Matthew 10:7-8, Jesus says, *As you go, proclaim this message: 'The kingdom of heaven has come near.' Heal the sick, raise the dead, cleanse those who have leprosy, drive out demons. Freely you have received; freely give*. The message of the cross, according to Kingdom Theology, must be preached with more than persuasive words [as the Apostle Paul mentioned in 1 Corinthians 4:20], but with a demonstration of the Spirit's power.

Though the Kingdom of God exists in this world in part, Kingdom Theology teaches that the devil rules this world. In John 12:31 Jesus said, *Now is the time for judgment on this world; now **the prince of this world** will be driven out*. In 2 Corinthians 4:4 Paul said, ***The god of this age*** *has blinded the minds of the unbelievers, so that they* *cannot see the light of the gospel that displays the glory of Christ, who is the image of God.* I love how Paul refers to satan as a little "g" god, and Jesus as the big "G" God. Satan may be the ruler of this Earth, but a little "g" never has as much authority as a big "G." With all of this being said, Kingdom Theologians teach that there is a spiritual battle for souls in this world between the powers of Heaven and the powers of darkness. In this spiritual battle, the righteous are not fighting *for* victory, but *from* victory. In Matthew 11:12 [KJV] Jesus says, *And from the days of John the Baptist until now the kingdom of heaven suffereth violence, and the violent take it by force.*

This verse is referring to the promises of God which are in Heaven that we want to become our reality. In that statement Jesus wasn't talking about actual violence occurring in Heaven, as there is no violence in Heaven. To explain what He meant, let's read Luke 17:21 [KJV]. Jesus said, *"Neither shall they say, Lo here! or, lo there! for, behold, the kingdom of God [Heaven] is within you."* Since we know that as Christians we are currently seated in heavenly places at the same time that we exist in this world, we have dual citizenship simultaneously on Earth *and* in Heaven. With the Kingdom of Heaven [in part] being within us, the violence that occurs doesn't actually happen in Heaven, but within this world.

Since the devil is the ruler of this world and we live in it, the spiritual battle is between us and Heaven. When Jesus said that the violent people would take it by force, He didn't mean that evil people would take over Heaven, because that doesn't make any sense. The violent people He is referring to are the righteous who trust in Him regardless of the situation. The righteous may suffer violence from demonic forces, but they forcefully grab hold of God's promises which releases deliverance through the supernatural power of the Holy Spirit. **They fight** in the *partial* Kingdom of Heaven, on Earth, **for**

what they know belongs to them from the *fully known* Kingdom of **Heaven**, in Heaven. To try and better explain this, the righteous declare the promises of God into existence that are not as though they were [Read Romans 4:17 KJV]. By force, this incredible act of faith declaration releases tangible promises from His reality into ours.

Kingdom Theology: Faith Healing

As I mentioned earlier, we are not living in the fullness of God's Kingdom while living on Earth. This is one reason we pray for the sick and not everyone is healed. There is a spiritual battle during divine healing that occurs between the demons and the prayer warriors. Even in Kingdom Theology, there is still a mystery in divine healing. What we do know is that Jesus commanded us to heal the sick. "Jesus didn't tell us to pray for the sick; He commanded us to heal them" as Bill Johnson says [Matthew 10:8]. It is *always* God's will to heal. In other words, Jesus didn't tell us to pray for healing only if it's God's will, He told us to heal the sick because it is His will. There is no theological explanation as to why God supernaturally removes a brain tumor from one person but allows another person to pass away. Ezekiel 18:32 says, *For I take no pleasure in the death of anyone, declares the Sovereign Lord. Repent and live!* Creating a theology for divine healing defeats the purpose of faith. It is impossible to whole heartedly trust God while expecting to have all the answers at the same time.

Why is it then that everyone doesn't get healed through prayer? My honest answer to that question is... I don't know. And I don't say that because you've stumped me, but because God has not given us the answer to that question. While I may not know why God doesn't heal every single sickness, I *do* know that I've seen Him do it before and I know He will do it again. Let's first look at Judges 6:12-14, *When the angel of the Lord appeared to Gideon, he said, "The Lord is with you mighty warrior."* **"Pardon me, my lord,"** *Gideon replied,* **"but if the Lord is with us, why has all this happened to us?** *Where are all his wonders that our ancestors told us about when they said, 'Did not the Lord bring us up out of Egypt?' But now the Lord has abandoned us and given us into the hand of Midian." The Lord turned to him and said, "Go in the strength you have and save Israel out of Midian's hand. Am I not sending you?"*

I find it interesting that God never answered Gideon's question. He simply told him to save Israel. Gideon, like many of us today, lost faith in the Lord's promises when bad things started to happen to him that he couldn't explain. The angel of the Lord, however, declared that God had been with him the whole time. To make sure that the Lord was speaking to him, Gideon put God to the test three times by asking for signs and wonders. We are not supposed to put God to the test according to Deuteronomy 6:16, but for some reason when asked nicely, God complies. *Then Gideon said to God, "Do not be angry with me. Let me make just one more request. Allow me one more test with the fleece, but this time make the fleece dry and let the ground be covered with dew." That night God did so. Only the fleece was dry; all the ground was covered with dew* [Judges 6:39-40]. God isn't pleased when we put Him to the test because it shows a lack of trust on our end. Still, the reason God grants our requests from time to time when we put Him to the test is because He wants us to build our faith in Him.

A Faith Healing Testimony

At my church after service on a Thursday night, I spotted an older woman whom I've prayed for in the past for healing. Curious to see how she was doing, my friend John and I made our way over to talk to her. For those of you that may not remember, she was the same older woman I mentioned at the very end of Chapter Four who was healed by faith of a severe neck injury that happened over twenty years ago. It had been several weeks, if not months, since Sal [my friend] and I prayed for her healing. The woman said that she was still healed and has not experienced any pain since the day we prayed for her.

Toward the end of our conversation, the woman said that she had pain on her side that was adjacent to her stomach. My friend suggested that we pray for her, and the woman replied, "Oh it's okay, don't worry about that. I've been prayed for before and that pain hasn't gone away. I've gotten used to it by now." My friend John was persistent, however, and said, "I believe God is going to heal you, do you mind if we lay hands on you? You're going to experience a miracle right now." Almost reluctantly, she accepted our invitation for prayer. John started the prayer, and I finished it off. We both prayed something similar to, "God, we pray in the name of Jesus that this pain be removed completely. There is no pain in Heaven, so we command Heaven's reality to become her reality right now in Jesus' name; zero pain right now in Jesus' name! We pray for your holy fire to consume the sickness in her body, burn it up, and restore her back to the way you created her to be."

At the same time, we were declaring that, the woman interrupted us and said, "I am actually feeling a warmth inside my body right now; that's pretty interesting." After the prayer, I asked her if she had any more pain there. She moved around for a few seconds, then said, "Yeah it's still there, but I appreciate you praying for me." Then I said, "I believe you're going to be healed completely even if it didn't happen right now. Be watchful; the Lord is going to heal you." As we started to walk away, the woman blurted out, "There's no more pain, there's no more pain at all! It's completely gone; this is incredible!" Sometimes God's healing doesn't happen right now. There are times when He heals the sick instantly, and other times He waits just a little longer to test our faith. It's all in His timing. My theology is to believe that God is healing the sick right now, not later. By believing that, I have seen a lot more miracles happening sooner rather than later.

If now isn't His timing, then we continue to have faith that He will heal when He chooses. If God chooses to not intervene through healing at all, instead of blaming God or trying to figure out why, we go back to the times when we know He did heal by faith and believe He will do it again. When I say there are times God chooses to not intervene through healing, I am not saying that God causes pain, suffering, or death. Jesus died on the cross, so we can live, not die. Death and diseases are the devil's doing and have nothing to do with God. Whenever a person doesn't get healed, it is false to assume that the devil has won by taking his/her life. The reality is that the devil has actually lost the spiritual war by taking the life of a believer, because that person goes to Heaven which is out of his reach forever. God has ultimate authority over life and death, and sometimes God chooses to raise the dead just to prove to the devil that *He* is in charge.

A Modern Day Lazarus

This true story begins with a Pastor named Daniel Ekechukwu who at the time resided in Onitsha Nigeria. On his way home after running an errand, Daniel was driving down a very steep hill. As his car started to gain speed, Daniel tried to apply the brake pedal, but to his surprise, it was inoperative. Daniel frantically continued pumping the pedal, but because of the brake failure, the car eventually accelerated to uncontrollable speeds and crashed into a large pillar on the side of the road. Daniel miraculously survived the head on collision, but lost consciousness and was vomiting large amounts of blood. Immediately after the collision, he was transported to a hospital in Owerri, Nigeria to receive medical treatment. On the way to the hospital, Daniel saw two angels of the Lord standing in the ambulance. Shortly after seeing the angels, Daniel passed away. After his death, Daniel says that the two angels escorted him to another angel of the Lord who told him, *"Right now, we are going to visit paradise."*

When Daniel arrived in Heaven, he saw all of the saints dressed in pure white robes singing praises and bowing down to the Lord. Daniel wanted to join them, but the angel of the Lord said, *"No, I still have a lot of things to show you; do not go in. Let us go and visit the Mansion that Jesus promised."* The mansion, as Daniel describes, was so glorious that it was indescribable with words. Then the angel of the Lord said, *"Jesus has finished the mansions, but the saints are not ready. Now let us visit hell."* When Daniel and the angel of the Lord arrived at the gates of hell, the angel waved his hand and the gates opened up. As soon as the gates opened, the people were screaming and asking Daniel for help. The angel of the Lord gave Daniel a paper and a pen to record all of the things he was witnessing. Daniel turned to the angel to ask for help, and the angel of the Lord replied, *"You have another chance to go back. The request of the rich man in hell has been granted to this generation."* The request of the rich man is in Luke 16:19-31.

To backtrack, after Daniel died in the ambulance, his body was taken to the mortuary on November 30th 2001. Daniel's wife could not believe what had just happened, and she refused to accept her husband's death as God's will, so she began to declare aloud God's promises. The promise she chose to declare was in Hebrews 11:35a, which says, *women received back their dead, raised to life again.* On December 2nd 2001, Daniel's wife convinced the mortician to release the body of her husband so that they could transport it to Reinhard Bonnke, a well-known evangelist who had been preaching at the time. She knew Bonnke to be a powerful man of God with great faith. Daniel's wife figured if she could only get her husband's body into the church where Bonnke was preaching, Jesus would resurrect him from the dead. The mortician secured Daniel's body in his coffin and then put the casket inside of an ambulance to be transported to Bonnke's healing conference. When the ambulance arrived at its destination, an usher from the church saw it and alerted two officials from the conference. The two officials talked with Daniel's wife and tried to convince her to not bring Daniels coffin into the church because it would be an embarrassment to the conference.

In the middle of that conversation, the conference security team rushed over to the ambulance and ordered that the coffin be opened to make sure it wasn't a bomb being brought into the church. When security realized that there really was a body in the coffin instead of a bomb, they ordered that the coffin be taken back to the mortuary. After hearing this, Daniel's wife began to cry out, [paraphrased] "I believe God is going to raise my husband from the dead; we need to get him into the church!" The security team argued with Daniel's wife for several minutes until they were finally convinced to allow the coffin to be brought into the church. Next, Daniel's body was removed from the coffin and carried into the church basement where they laid his body down on top of a table. Shortly after laying his body down, Daniel started breathing.

When everyone saw this, two pastors began immediately to pray for his complete healing. After a while, word spread throughout the church that a man who had been dead for three days was now breathing again. People from the church were shouting and trying to get into the basement to see what was happening. At the same time the people in the basement heard the shouting, Daniel came to life and jumped up from the table while gasping for air. Daniel, over the next few days, smelled of embalming fluid from the injections at the mortuary, but later continued to live a normal life. This is a true story from a viral video titled, "Raised from the Dead" by Evangelist Reinhard Bonnke [to learn more about this video, go to http://www.cbn.com/700club/features/bonnke_raisedpastor.aspx].

There are many other true stories out there similar to this, but the point I want to make through this story is that Jesus has all authority both on Earth and in Heaven. The devil may be the sheriff of the Earth, but God is the Judge of the universe; the Lord has the final say over life and death.

I honestly must say that I am very thankful to John Wimber for reviving the faith of American citizens by founding The Signs and Wonders Movement. Wimber didn't bring signs and wonders back to life for the world [as miracles have always been happening in other countries since the beginning of man-kind], but he brought faith in God's supernatural power back to life in America. While I do believe in signs, wonders, and the supernatural, I will admit there are some charismatic Christians out there believing things that are against the Word of God. Let's take a look at one of these bizarre groups.

False Doctrine

There is a small, charismatic group that emerged in the 60's from The Latter Rain Movement. The Latter Rain Movement in itself aligns with the Word of God, but the particular branch I am describing that emerged from their organization is wrong in its teachings. One of the strange teachings of this small-branched organization was formulated in the early 70's. The leader of the organization at that time began preaching heavily on the End Times. His message taught that Christians needed to move into the wilderness in preparation for Christ's return. Believing every word he said, many of his followers quit their jobs and moved their families to rural areas. The Bible says we are to be followers of Jesus, not followers of man. If you want to live in the wilderness and eat wild berries for breakfast, lunch, and dinner, that's up to you, but let's not teach people that Jesus wants us to do that when it's not in the Bible.

Sinless Perfection

The same organization later formulated an idea of sinless living which is based on the Apostle Paul's "Dead to Sin" excerpt from the book of Romans; the teaching stated that sinless living is the goal for all Christians, and if there is any sin in our lives, we are not truly saved. The truth is that we are saved by grace alone, as Scripture states. While the Bible does say that Jesus lived a life without sin, it doesn't say that our primary goal is to be perfect because then we are trying to perform. The spirit of performance is a killer in the Body of Christ today. Having perfection be the goal of our Christian lifestyle puts our eyes on each other and takes them off Jesus. Sinless living is not the goal for all Christians; our goal is to draw people closer to God's heart. If we are constantly pointing the finger at one another in a comparison to see who's closer to perfection, we won't have any time to show anyone the love of God.

When Jesus died on the cross, He died to sin once and for all and made us slaves to righteousness rather than slaves to sin [Romans

6:15-18]. For believers, His death on the cross killed sin and made us righteous. Adam and Eve were unaware of sin [like Jesus] prior to eating from the tree of knowledge, but after eating from the tree they were ashamed to be naked. As soon as Adam and Eve ate from the tree of knowledge, they felt shame which was the first indicator of the sin nature. Jesus' death for our sins takes us back in time to the days of Adam and Eve before they had eaten from the tree of knowledge of good and evil. That is how God sees us today: as righteous saints. Like Adam and Eve, however, being righteous saints doesn't mean that we cannot choose to sin. Jesus may have removed our sin nature, but not our freewill. Every day as Christians, we make Adam and Eve decisions by choosing whether or not we are going to eat from the tree of knowledge [sin] or from Christ's tree of righteousness. When it comes down to it, God doesn't care if people want to try and live without sin. The most important thing we need to know is that our salvation is not dependent on what we do, but it has been secured by what He did.

For those analytical thinkers like myself, it is important for us to understand the history of God's signs and wonders so that there can be somewhat of a connection between our heads and our hearts. For some of us, when our heads understand that miracles have been happening after the Bible's completion until now, it makes it a little easier for our hearts to believe they can happen for us. God not only gave us intelligence so that we can study the Bible and learn about His power and love, but He also gave us hearts to experience both of those attributes. As we learn to transform our minds to align with His thinking, we will finally realize that we are worthy of inheriting His supernatural gifts. Next, we are going to learn how to recognize and expel false humility.

Chapter Ten
The Spirit of False Humility

The Poverty-Stricken Mindset [Part 1]

The Spirit of Poverty

In The Old Testament days, we were sinners saved by our works. For example, sacrificing animals was required as atonement for sin to maintain our righteousness. I bring that up because a lot of the poverty-stricken thoughts today come from the Old Testament. Before Jesus died on the cross, righteousness was something we had to work for. But after God raised Jesus from the dead, our righteousness was no longer based on our performance, but it was solidified by God's grace. I believe that the idea of having to work for righteousness [which is Old Testament theology] is one reason many Christians are living in spiritual poverty.

When Jesus died on the cross, we became dead to poverty, meaning we shouldn't be continuing to view ourselves as *not good enough*. To call ourselves not good enough is an insult to God because He never makes mistakes. What we believe about ourselves in our spirit becomes the truth in our reality. In order for us to believe in God's supernatural power, we need to first make sure that we believe we're worthy of it.

We Are Not Sinners Saved by Grace

"We are sinners saved by grace" is an unbiblical teaching that has been circulating within Christianity for many years. Saying that I'm a sinner saved by grace is the same as saying, "I'm glad the Lord saved me, because Him and I both know I'm nothin' but a piece a garbage." If the last three words from this saying are removed, it would say "we are sinners." We may have been saved by the grace of God, but if we still see ourselves as low-life sinners, that's how we're going to act. People who think this way truly believe they're being humble, but it's actually false humility. The best way for me to explain the way we should view ourselves in Christ is stated by a man named Charles Hodge. He said, "The doctrines of grace humble a man without degrading him and exalt a man without inflating him." Now rearranging the "sinners saved by grace" statement to become relevant to Christians today, it would say, "We *were* sinners saved before grace, but because of it we are righteous" [Philippians 3:9].

The reason I keep bringing up the feeling of not being good enough is because this was a feeling I struggled with my entire life until the Lord brought Elizabeth Reisinger and Eric Waterbury [two very powerful leaders within my local church and the Bethel Church community] into my life to teach me otherwise. To backtrack, after high school, my life went downhill. Suicide was a thought that crossed my mind almost on a daily basis. One warm, lonely night while I was living in Orlando, I decided to go to church. I showed up at church extremely depressed with intense feelings of unworthiness. Toward the end of the service, everyone went to the front of the church to hold hands in prayer. When I turned around to hold the hands of the people standing next to me, they were already holding the hands of other people. It appeared to me that I was the only person not holding someone's hand. As I looked around for someone's hand to hold, people looked at me as though I didn't belong there; I felt like an outcast. While today I realize that I was probably making a bigger deal out of that situation than it really was, my feelings of worthlessness back then only heightened when I wasn't acknowledged during prayer time.

"I am going to kill myself tonight; I have nothing else to live for" I thought to myself, holding back the tears. After the service, I put on a fake smile for everyone as I quickly left the building to head to my car. Now, out of everyone's sight, tears endlessly began to stream down my face. As I headed toward the highway, I heard a voice in my head tell me, "Tonight is the night you will die." I started to hear demonic voices of people screaming. It was difficult to focus on driving because the demonic visions were extremely vivid. Keep in mind this experience I had was prior to me believing in God's power. While I may not have believed in the power of God at that time, I did believe in the power of the devil. Getting back to the story, as I drove onto the highway I heard the voice in my head say, "All you need to do is crash your car head-on into the center divider, and all the pain will go away forever." After hearing that voice, I floored the gas pedal.

The more I gained speed, the more vivid the visions became. I started hearing gun shots and saw many pictures of knives. At a certain point after breaking one-hundred miles an hour, I started swerving in and out of traffic in hopes that I would lose control of the car and die. I maintained this speed for about thirty seconds but miraculously didn't lose control. Eventually I did make it home safely which I didn't understand, but God did. The reason I share this is because I want everyone to know how dangerous the spirit of poverty can become. Not feeling good enough for anything or anyone eventually leads to suicide; it's only a matter of time.

Whether we believe it or not, we need to realize as humans that we are not fighting against flesh and blood as the Apostle Paul said, but against demonic forces. By not believing in His power, we can never beat the spirit of poverty. As Christ followers, however, we have already won the battle even before it began. One way that I was able to step out of my spiritual poverty was by getting away from other Christians who had the same spirit. Surrounding yourself with other believers who are righteous tends to rub off on you.

Spiritual Poverty Inherited Through Generational Curses

Leviticus 26:39-42 says: Those of you who are left will waste away in the lands of their enemies because of their sins; **also because of their ancestors' sins they will waste away.** "'But if they will confess their sins and the sins of their ancestors—their unfaithfulness and their hostility toward me, I will remember my covenant with Jacob and my covenant with Isaac and my covenant with Abraham, and I will remember the land.'" Though this was written in the Old Testament Book of the Law which was abolished, many people today suffer from the sins of their ancestors and forget that Jesus already broke that chain to the past. Jesus has given Christians authority to break generational curses through the power of the Holy Spirit. It is no longer necessary to live in poverty caused by our ancestors because we have been given authority through Christ to break that chain. Many times, we inherit generational curses from our ancestors without realizing it.

There was a boy from my grade school days named Brandon who was notorious for getting into trouble. He was considered to be a low-class thug by many of the other children in my class. Brandon was always arguing with his teachers to prove that he was the boss.

The reason he did that was because it was entertaining to the other classmates and it drew a lot of attention to himself--attention he wasn't receiving from his parents at home. Children growing up need attention. Growing up in an attention-starved environment, leaves children starving for attention for the rest of their lives. One day, Brandon's parents decided to show up to the classroom uninvited. Brandon had been lying to his parents and told them that his teacher was mistreating him verbally, so they were furious as they entered the classroom. Within only a few minutes, Brandon's parents were screaming profanity at the teacher to defend their son. It was obvious that day to everyone in the classroom, including myself, that Brandon had inherited his behavior from his parents.

On another day of school during a second confrontation between Brandon and his teacher, Brandon threatened to hit his teacher if she didn't leave him alone. The teacher told him that if he didn't apologize for his threat, she would need to expel him from the school district. Brandon however refused to apologize, and that day he was expelled. Brandon never saw himself as good enough to finish school due to his poverty mentality. The poverty minded person often feels that they got the short end of the stick when they were born, therefore they think that they are predestined to live a life of perpetual paralysis. People who have this type of victim mentality often believe in fate. According to "The Free Dictionary by Farlex," fate is defined as: The supposed force, principle, or power that predetermines events.

The truth is that "the supposed force" described in The Free Dictionary is your mind. People like Brandon fail to break the curse of poverty inherited from their ancestors by believing, "If my family wasn't good enough, then I'm not good enough either." If our parents didn't feel worthy of God's love or didn't believe in the supernatural, we will be cursed with the same wrong thinking unless we become transformed by the renewing of our minds. If you can think it, through Christ, you do it! [Philippians 4:13] Freewill, along with being taught the truth, enables us to defeat the spirit of poverty when we choose to view ourselves as His righteous sons/daughters. Forgiving the sins of our ancestors plays a huge role in helping many of us to see ourselves as righteous rather than sinners.

Forgiveness Breaks the Curse

The supernatural power of forgiveness is strong enough to break generational curses. Scripture tells us that forgiveness is so important, that God won't forgive our sins if we don't forgive the sins of others. By not forgiving others for what they have done to us, we are locking ourselves inside a prison of bitterness and resentment. The people who you don't forgive are living happy lives and they're doing just great, but you're still angry about how much they've hurt you. By holding unforgiveness in your heart, you're quenching the power of God. Sometimes a person doesn't get physically healed by God not because He didn't want to do it, but because the unforgiveness hidden inside of that person disabled God's power. I have heard testimonies from very close friends of mine who have had this experience. As soon as your unforgiveness is released, His healing comes.

Forgiving others is not a natural human instinct, but revenge is. Revenge is definitely a fruit of a spirit, but a rotten one. It may not seem fair to Christians that we are to forgive those who do us wrong instead of retaliating, but that's only because revenge is not up to us, it's up to the Lord. *Do not take revenge, my dear friends, but leave room for Gods wrath, for it is written: "It is mine to avenge; I will repay," says the Lord* [Romans 12:19]. When Jesus tells you to turn the other cheek, it's not because He wants people to beat you up, it's because He's got a surprise for your enemy when he decides to try and hit you again. Now to discourage people who think it's okay to pray for revenge on their enemies, Proverbs 24:17-18 says, *Do not gloat when your enemy falls; when they stumble, do not let your heart rejoice, or the Lord will see and disapprove and turn his wrath away from them.*

A few years ago, there was a coworker at my job whom I wasn't very fond of, and I wasn't the only one. This coworker became the top selling salesperson in our district by stealing commissioned sales from all of the other associates including myself. This continued to go on for about a year. During that time, the other associates and I decided to save our commission documents in hopes that the corrupt associate would get caught. Several times we would turn in our documents to our managers, but the managers looked the other way. Then we decided to turn in our documents to loss prevention, but loss prevention told us that there was nothing they could do to help us. In frustration, I began to contemplate hiring a lawyer to sue the corrupt associate for lost wages. In the middle of my frustration, I heard a subtle voice tell me, *"What are you doing son?"* I knew the Lord was convicting me. I stopped researching lawyers and began to weep. The Lord, through both direct revelation and advice from friends and family, was telling me to pray for the corrupt coworker.

After almost a whole year of fighting him in the natural for what rightfully belonged to me, I began to fight in the spirit. I prayed blessings over his family and peace in the work environment between him, myself, and the other associates. One day at work after praying for him, I noticed that he was being unusually nice. In fact, he was so nice, that one of my female associates asked him, "Dude, what's wrong with you, why are you so nice today?" The corrupt associate answered, "I don't know, I just feel like today is a good day." He didn't realize that the supernatural power of God was influencing his mind. This unusually nice behavior in him continued for a few months, until he eventually started going back to his old ways. God had the power to permanently transform his mind, but He [God] didn't do it because He gives him [the corrupt associate], along with you and I, a freewill. When the associate's corrupted behavior returned, my faith started to grow weary.

Then just before I gave up on the Lord's promises, there was a breakthrough. On the last day of the year, the corrupt salesperson was fired. I was rejoicing not because he lost his job, but because the Lord had delivered me, and I'd won the battle. I prayed that the Lord would bless his family and that somehow someway, God would speak to him and turn the man's heart towards the Lord. To this day I have forgiven the man for what he did to me. It doesn't matter what your enemies do to you, forgiving them of their sins breaks the curse of poverty. Jesus ultimately broke the curse of poverty by asking God to forgive the men who nailed Him to the cross. His act of forgiveness along with His devout obedience to the Lord raised Him from the dead just as He had prophesied. Forgiveness through Christ has a supernatural ability to destroy the curse of poverty and raise people who are living, as though dead, to life.

Something important to know is that forgiveness is **not** a two-way street. Forgiveness starts and ends with you. Apologizing when you're wrong also aids in the destruction of spiritual poverty both for yourself and for the other person. If you have hurt someone, apologizing to the other person will help him/her to heal from the pain. If the other person doesn't forgive you for what you have done, that unforgiveness is now between that person and the Lord. Apologizing sets *you* free from your iniquities. Forgiving someone who doesn't deserve it and apologizing when you're wrong may seem like weakness to a foolish man, but they're signs of strength in the eyes of the Lord. When you forgive your offender and view that person the way Jesus does, you no longer see yourself as: not good enough, incompetent, slow, or poor. People who call you those names are actually struggling with negative emotions they've repressed since their own childhood. Your offender is only repeating with you what they have inherited from their ancestors. *You* have the ability to break the curse; your spiritual poverty can end right now through the power of Jesus Christ! When He said, *"It is finished,"* He meant it.

Confidence Masquerades as Arrogance to the Insecure

Jealousy and insecurity are two common characteristics of poverty minded individuals. Many Christians and non-Christians alike love to criticize pastors who are extremely wealthy. While I agree that it's not okay for a pastor to flaunt his riches like a high profile, secular rapper, there is nothing wrong with being blessed. People who view themselves as unworthy become insecure and jealous when God blesses others in the natural realm. Viewing yourself as righteous has nothing to do with arrogance, but what it means is that you see yourself as awesome only because He is awesome. Jesus lived as the poor did so that He could develop a relationship with us by lowering Himself to our level. He died a life of poverty so that we would live life in abundance.

How amazing is our God to stoop down to our level just to become intimate with us and make us righteous through His Son. I find that mind-blowing! In saying that, we need to make sure we are not living a lifestyle of poverty through false humility to try and make ourselves righteous. We're insulting the creator of the universe when we try to do something that He already did! When we finally break free from the spirit of poverty, the Lord will bless us with more of His love which shuts the door on skepticism and enables us to encounter His presence. Now that we understand the meaning of false humility, let's take a look at what true humility is all about.

Chapter Eleven
Walking in the Footsteps of Jesus

The True Humility of Being Poor in Spirit [Part 2]

Preface [Divine Inspiration]

Initially, I had no plans to write a Part Two about the spirit of poverty, but the Lord convicted me through two visions. The Lord wrecked me so much during the visions that I've decided to share them for His glory and our edification. It all started when I asked the Lord for revelation regarding some of the final subjects of this book. In the first vision, during prayer, I saw an image of a "W." I continued praying and the letter "W" completed into the word "wind." I still didn't understand what God was trying to say, so I continued praying. In the second vision was a picture of a flag. The flag had purple and yellow horizontal stripes, and it was flapping erratically from what appeared to be high winds. After the second vision, I decided to go on the internet and look up the flag's meaning. When the search results showed up, there was only one flag that had the same appearance as the one in my vision. With anticipation, I clicked the website linked to the flag to obtain more information about it.

The flag was described on the website to have been a fictional flag, but there was no additional explanation for it. Adjacent to the flag was an image of a document. I opened the document to find a letter written in German. Since I don't understand German, I almost gave up until I noticed that at the end of the letter were the words "Amen." Subsequently, I started to realize that the Lord had me on a personal treasure hunt. Next, I decided to translate the title of the German letter by using my web browser. The title of the letter was *"Gebeine des Heiligen Franziskus von Assisi,"* which in English translates to "The Remains of Saint Francis of Assisi." I researched Saint Francis because I knew very little about the history of Catholicism or saints, and I came to realize that he was a charismatic Catholic who had a passionate relationship with Jesus. As a side note: Saint Francis prophesied, healed the sick, and cast out many demons by the power of Christ throughout his ministry. One of his famous quotes that I read *after* creating the title of this chapter was, "To follow the teachings of our Lord Jesus Christ and to walk in his footsteps." Many Christians nowadays don't know what it truly means to live for Christ. This chapter is going to open our eyes to the true meaning of Christianity.

Saint Francis of Assisi

Saint Francis honored the lifestyle of Jesus so much that he even imitated the poverty of Christ. As I mentioned at the end of the previous chapter, living a life of poverty is not required as Jesus already did it for us, but I truly honor this man for *choosing* to live in poverty for the purpose of drawing people to the heart of God; it's a beautiful thing. At a certain point, I began to ask the Lord why He wanted me to learn all of these things about Saint Francis. Then the Lord said to me, *"I want my people today to honor me the same way Saint Francis did. My people need to know what it really means to live for Christ; undiluted."* Saint Francis didn't have a spirit of poverty, but he was truly poor in spirit. He knew who he was in Christ to the point where he operated in probably all of the spiritual gifts with confidence and authority, but he was also a very humble man who always pointed to Christ in all of his works. One of the many things I find amazing about St. Francis is that he is not known for walking in God's supernatural power, but he is known for his big heart for the poor; that was his focus. There is a difference between having a spirit of poverty and being poor in spirit. They sound similar, but they have completely different meanings.

The spirit of poverty is inspired by 2 Corinthians 8:9. The verse says, For you know the grace of our Lord Jesus Christ, that though he was rich, yet for your sake he became poor, so that you through his poverty might become rich. When this verse is interpreted incorrectly, it means that we are required to live in poverty like Jesus so that other people who are better than we are will become rich through our hardship. There is nothing wrong with choosing to live in poverty if our hearts are in the right place like Saint Francis, but thinking that it's required to live in poverty is an insult to the Lord. The term "poor in spirit" [on the other hand] is explained in Matthew 5:3 which says, Blessed are the poor in spirit, for theirs is the kingdom of heaven. Jesus doesn't bless us when we think less of ourselves, He blesses us when we think more of Him.

It is possible to be both rich and poor in spirit at the same time. In the natural, these words contradict each other because we think about money, but in the Spirit, rich is defined by our righteousness in Christ and poor is the definition of true humility and surrender. We are only rich in Spirit because of our poor-like dependency on Christ alone. Jesus is the perfect example of this. Just because Jesus lived a humble life in poverty didn't mean He was unaware of His God DNA. In John 13:13-14 Jesus said, *"You call me 'Teacher' and 'Lord,' and rightly so, for that is what I am. Now that I, your Lord and Teacher, have washed your feet, you also should wash one another's feet."*

This verse clearly shows what being a righteous saint who is poor [humble] in spirit should look like. I believe that Missionary Heidi Baker stated the definition of "poor in spirit" perfectly when she said, "I believe Jesus meant that poor in spirit is a posturing of the heart where one is wholly given, fully yielded, completely desperate, and totally dependent on God alone."

The Poverty of Christ

As Christians, being poor in spirit has a few meanings. It doesn't specifically mean having a low income, but it means to have our hearts completely surrendered to God. It means we give all of ourselves to Him because we don't have a back-up plan. He gave His life for what He believed in: love. If we truly love Jesus, we need to be willing to do the same for Him. *Whoever does not take up their cross and follow me is not worthy of me. Whoever finds their life will lose it, and whoever loses their life for my sake will find it* [Matthew 10-38-39]. What this verse means is that we need to be willing to die for Him if it really came down to it. We need to give all of ourselves to Him by living solely for Christ. A wife would not be very happy if her husband only visited with her once in a while to show his love for her; that's not very convincing. When you give fifty percent of yourself to your spouse, you have a fifty percent chance that your marriage will continue in a healthy manner. Fifty percent might not sound too bad, but on a grade school test it means we've failed miserably. Being married to Christ, we need to give all of ourselves to Him in everything we do. When we give all of ourselves to Him as the end of the verse says, we will find the true meaning of life in abundance.

Living poor in spirit also means to be willing to associate with people of low status according to the world's standards, not because we are better than them, but because we are the same. *"The Son of Man came eating and drinking, and they say, 'Here is a glutton and a drunkard, a friend of tax collectors and sinners.' But wisdom is proved right by her deeds* [Matthew 11:19]." Now Jesus obviously wasn't a drunkard or a glutton, but when we truly start to live for Christ, religious people will create false accusations about us to feed the appetite of their self-righteousness. In the Bible days, living for Christ was a pretty extreme lifestyle because those Christians were often persecuted. One of many reasons they were persecuted was because they were falsely accused of crimes they didn't commit. Today, many Christians in other countries are living in poverty because the law does not allow them to live any other way. It's easy to live for Christ when there is no opposition. The day we choose to follow Christ while being fully aware that we could lose our lives because of our faith, is the day we begin to walk in the footsteps of Jesus.

Christians in the Middle East

The Middle East is notorious for Christian persecution by Muslim extremists. In many Middle Eastern countries, it is against the law to be a Christian, and anyone who follows Jesus is considered to be an infidel. Christians who live there are considered to be low-class citizens and are treated poorly by the majority of the population. Throughout my studies on the religion of Islam, the Lord wanted me to have a better understanding of their beliefs, and He also wanted my heart to break for the persecuted Christians living in Islamic countries. As a Christian in Pakistan, for example, it is dangerous to go to church because they never know when it will be raided by the authorities. Christians have been splashed with acid, beheaded, severely fined, and tortured in many other ways because they've chosen to follow Jesus. Many Christians there live in isolated communities so they can avoid the dangers of life in the city. Bibles are not easy to come by in those countries either. Many Christians hide their Bibles and meet in underground locations to worship God. One of the most fascinating things that I honor in Middle Eastern Christians despite all the persecution taking place, is their hearts.

Jesus said in Matthew 5:43-44, "You have heard that it was said, 'Love your neighbor and hate your enemy.' But I tell you, love your enemies and pray for those who persecute you." Middle Eastern Christians show love in their hearts for their enemies even when their houses are burned down, they love them when their families are kidnapped, and siblings are raped and killed, and they love them when they don't receive that love in return. To love anyone under these extreme conditions is to genuinely have the heart of God. Many of us don't know what it's like to live under these conditions; we don't understand what it really means to take up our crosses and follow Him. It's amazing to me, however, that many Christians in the Mid-East know that they're rich because of what Jesus did for them. They don't look at their situations and say, "I've got a problem," they look at their Creator and say, "We've got a problem." Despite all of the persecution taking place, there are many amazing testimonies happening in these countries.

Signs and Wonders in the Middle East

Ramadan is the name of an intense period of fasting that Muslims participate in once a year. Muslims pray to Allah for direction in their lives and for the general well-being of their families. One of the most amazing things that happen during Ramadan is that many Muslims have reported seeing visions of Jesus. One of the qualities of the Muslim lifestyle, despite my disagreement with their beliefs, is that they have a child-like faith. Most Muslims who convert to Christianity during Ramadan do so because Jesus spoke to them in a vision or a dream. They won't believe if Christians try to convince them that Christ is the way, but they will believe if Christ Himself tells them. In one instance, I know of a former Muslim woman [who converted to Christianity] who was reading the Bible in her room one night. Then, suddenly out of nowhere, a very bright light entered the room. The woman saw Jesus enter her room, and He talked to her about a personal situation going on in her life. This sounds like a story out of the Bible, but these things happen on a regular basis for them. Charismatic Christians are not labeled in those countries because most, if not all Christians living there encounter the tangible power and love of God on a regular basis.

For both Muslims and Christians living in the Middle East, there is a child-like faith that we can learn from as believers living in other parts of the world. Something I find interesting is that miracles of God happen more often in Third World countries than they do in America. Why is it that there are resurrections from the dead happening in poverty-stricken areas, but not in other wealthier places like our country? I believe that when Jesus said, *blessed are the poor in spirit for theirs is the kingdom of heaven*, He meant that people who are poor in spirit will possess His Kingdom on Earth. In addition to this, Jesus said in Matthew 19:30, *But many who are first will be last, and many who are last will be first*. Jesus said this more than once in the Bible, and both times He was saying that the poor in spirit would see Heaven before the rich. As a side note, I don't believe there is anything wrong with being rich, but with that being said, the poor in spirit [the "last" that Jesus referred to] will see Heaven come to Earth before the wealthy will. As I mentioned earlier, being poor in spirit doesn't necessarily mean living in poverty. Missionary Heidi Baker is a perfect example of this.

Miracles in Mozambique

Heidi Baker, along with her husband Rolland, are co-founders of Iris ministries which is known worldwide for its miracles. She was questioned once on why it is that miracles appear to happen more among the poor, and her response was, "They're so childlike in their belief. They just see way more. They're also more desperate, and they're more hungry in the natural realm; so it seems to pull the Kingdom of Heaven to them in a greater way." The Baker's headquarters is located in Pemba, Mozambique. Heidi Baker is a very well-educated woman with a PhD in systematic theology, but she chooses to live her life among the poor because of her big heart for the lost.

In June of 2014, I had the privilege to go on a mission trip to Pemba, Mozambique with Iris Ministries. While in Pemba, I witnessed four deaf people hear, one blind man see, and food supernaturally multiply. One early morning during our bush outreach in a village near Pemba, Heidi was serving all of the missionaries Starbucks coffee and tea. During that time, I got a chance to talk with her for a bit. Heidi told me that she personally drives to Starbucks, which is nowhere near Mozambique, and buys coffee and tea for all of her missionaries as a way to honor them. To this day, I continue to be amazed by the size of Heidi's heart, and I hope that one day I will be able to display God's love to others as well as she does. While many of us would love to see the dead raised and the cripple walk, it's actually the little things that God does in our lives through other people that will have the greatest impact on our hearts. God's intention for performing miracles isn't so that He can show us how powerful He is, but His desire through them is to show us how loved we are by Him.

Being poor in spirit, as Heidi often mentions, is more of a heart condition than it is anything else. The Bible says the heart has the ability to think. On that note, once we align our heart's thought process to the heart cries of the poor, we will begin to see His Kingdom come to Earth in a richer sense. To become rich in the Spirit requires us to position our hearts in a way that it thinks and sees the way Jesus does. Many of us living in wealthy environments have either never seen a miracle or see very little of them because our broken hearts have taught us that being poor in spirit is a punishment from God for all of the wrong things we've done. The spirit of poverty has told a lot of us that we aren't good enough to experience God's power the way the poor do, because the Lord loves the poor more than He loves the wealthy. When a brokenhearted person believes the lies of the spirit of poverty, those lies become the truth. Obviously, God doesn't favor the poor over the rich, but He *does* manifest more of himself to them because they're hearts are more open to an encounter with His love. The faith of the poor is insurmountable.

God created us to have a hunger for His presence. When we feed our appetites for Jesus with anything other than Him, a broken heart is the repercussion of that. A broken heart is unable to experience the wonders of God because it can't see past its poor-spirited condition, but when that broken heart has been healed, it's able to think and see the way Jesus did. The healed heart is not only capable of accepting His rich promises [which feeds our spiritual hunger], but it also manifests Heaven on Earth in greater measure due to its enlightenment. The poor in spirit with healed hearts are constantly being fed because their appetites are never satisfied with knowing God in part; they're always hungry for more. The hungrier we get, the richer we become, and the more we see Heaven's realm become normal in our lives.

The heart is a human organ the Bible talks a lot about, and there is a reason for that. Many people are walking around every day with broken hearts and they don't even realize it. When the heart is broken, one tends to operate in brokenness. Backtracking a little to chapter ten of this book, the spirit of poverty originates from a broken heart. Brokenhearted, poverty-minded individuals are usually in denial when asked about their erratic behaviors. They have gotten so comfortable with their brokenness, they think it's normal. The heart is the root of where all human intentions are birthed, and it's where our connection with God should be founded. A person with a broken heart is neither capable of experiencing the love of God nor His supernatural power since His power is a manifestation of His love. Healing for the brokenhearted is not only essential to experience the miraculous, but to also truly encounter His love which is the most amazing spiritual gift of all. If we truly want to step out of the spirit of poverty and into being poor in spirit, we need to make sure our hearts are healed and in the right place. In order to walk like Jesus, our hearts need to think like His.

Chapter Twelve
He Heals the Brokenhearted

Love Mends the Broken Heart

People who are skeptical of the supernatural are disbelieving because they're probably skeptical of love. If God is love and God is perfect, then His heart is also perfect. In His perfect heart, there is no such thing as brokenness. The only way possible for us to receive healing for our hearts is for us to go after God's heart which is perfect and pure. King David wasn't able to kill giants by simply being a great man, but by being a great man after God's own heart. This might be a harsh reality to many people, but if you don't believe in love, you don't believe in God, because God is love. True love comes from His pure heart being intertwined with ours. Since His perfect love is the foundation of the supernatural Gifts of the Spirit, I will define love so that those of us that are brokenhearted will see who God *really* is.

Love is patient, love is kind. It does not envy, it does not boast, it is not proud. It does not dishonor others, it is not self-seeking, it is not easily angered, it keeps no record of wrongs. Love does not delight in evil but rejoices with the truth. It always protects, always trusts, always hopes and always perseveres. Love never fails [1 Corinthians 13: 4-8a].

Love is patient. Patience means to wait on the Lord's timing for His will in our lives. Patience doesn't give one an excuse to be lazy, but it teaches an assertive individual how to persevere through faith when it looks like nothing is changing. Patience is not something my younger generation is fond of. We want everything right now. The older, more experienced generation has learned throughout their years of pain, trial, and error that doing it yourself doesn't work. But the younger generation, thinking they know better, repeats the same mistakes over and over again. I have been guilty of this myself, but my goal is to enlighten my younger generation by explaining the benefits of patience, which is transferable through the wisdom of our forefathers. The younger generation must learn from their elders how to apply the divine art of waiting on the Lord because patience really is a virtue.

Love is kind. To be kind means to treat others the way you want to be treated. People who operate in brokenness are often treated like garbage by their loved ones, so they treat others the same way and think that it's normal. What's normal is treating others kindly regardless of how they treat you in return because that's what Jesus meant when He told us to turn the other cheek.

It [love] does not envy; it is not envious of other people's success. There is a verse in the book of Matthew chapter six verse thirty-three [KJV] that says, *But seek ye first the kingdom of God, and his righteousness; and all these things shall be added unto you.* From that verse, Bill Johnson once stated, "Many Christians praise the one who seeks first the Kingdom but despise the one whom all things are added." Being jealous of others and/or trying to make someone jealous has nothing to do with love. Being jealous of God's blessings being poured upon His people who have stewarded what they've been given is called the spirit of stupid.

Love is not boastful, proud, or dishonoring. It's okay to be proud of yourself when accomplishing something great, but it's not okay to demean other people who haven't accomplished much. Dishonoring people by puffing ourselves up creates a disconnect between us and God because love cannot coexist with arrogance.

Love is not self-seeking. Many people enter into a relationship for the wrong reasons. People believe the primary reason they're in a relationship is to receive love; that's wrong. Receiving love is an obvious benefit to being in a relationship, but giving love is the main purpose of it. I find it fascinating that the Bible says the man is the head of the household, yet it also tells men to submit to their wives. Looking to receive love without any intention of reciprocating it sucks the life out of people. Love is intended to be given the same way we received it from Christ.

Love is not easily angered and keeps no record of wrongs. Being angry is not a sin but being easily angered is. *"In your anger do not sin": Do not let the sun go down while you are still angry* [Ephesians 4:26]. If a car cuts you off in traffic and the first thing you do is pull out a gun, you might have a problem. I believe that the issues of anger and keeping a record of wrongs were both mentioned within the same sentence in the book of Corinthians for a reason. Keeping a record of another person's wrongs and then continually throwing those bad records in his/her face only pours gasoline on the fire. We are all guilty of doing this at times, but we need to realize that there will never be a resolution as long as both individuals believe the other person is wrong. By keeping a record of another person's wrongs, we're also keeping a record of that person's sins, which is a sin in itself. God won't forgive our sins if we hold another man's sins against him.

Love does not delight in evil, but rejoices with the truth; love protects, trusts, hopes, and perseveres. When God's wrath comes upon our enemies, we are not to rejoice when they suffer, but we rejoice in our deliverance. God's love protects us from the hands of our enemies. Trusting and hoping in the Lord alone strengthens us in our difficult times. If a person has a reputation for being dishonest, love doesn't mean to blindly trust that person. Rather, love means to trust a person who is producing good fruit. *But the fruit of the Spirit is love, joy, peace, forbearance, kindness, goodness, faithfulness, gentleness and self-control. Against such things there is no law* [Galatians 5:22–23].

Love Never Fails

While there is such a thing as infatuation upon initial appearance, there is no such thing as love at first sight. A relationship fails early on when its foundation is built solely on outward appearance. *But the Lord said to Samuel, "Do not consider his appearance or his height, for I have rejected him. The Lord does not look at the things people look at. People look at the outward appearance, but the Lord looks at the heart* [1Samuel 16:7]." There is no such thing as falling out of love unless one falls into it first. Love is not something that "just happens;" love is a choice. The state of love is permanent; it never fails. People who say they don't believe in love are skeptical because they've had a bad experience. The reason I went through the trouble of explaining in such great detail the definition of love from the book of Corinthians is so that we will know what true love looks like.

Something I also want to mention after saying that, is that pure love comes from the heart of God which is perfect. Since we are not living in perfection, it is impossible for any human being to meet all of the criteria Paul talked about. At times, I am certainly guilty of being some of the things love should not be, but the most important part of love is that it never fails. Marriage symbolizes our oneness with Christ in which we become inseparable with Him. Mark 10:7-9 says, *'For this reason a man will leave his father and mother and be united to his wife, and the two will become one flesh.' So they are no longer two, but one flesh. Therefore, what God has joined together, let no one separate.* If both spouses are after God's heart alone, then marriage, like love, never fails. God designed marriage to unify us to our significant other until death. The same unconditional love we have for our spouse is the same love Christ has for us.

A Christ-centered marriage accompanied by good communication, setting boundaries, healthy confrontation, wise counseling [Matthew 18:15–16], and a willingness to repent when one is wrong [this applies equally to both spouses], will reap a love between the two that will never fail. When we pursue God's heart, this act allows us to bring the true meaning of love from Heaven down to Earth. If we start chasing after God's Heart the way King David did, the things in our hearts that contradict His nature become burned by the fire of the Holy Spirit. His fire purifies the deceitful heart of man [as Jeremiah 17:9 talks about] until it looks like the heart of God. After His cleansing within us is complete, we begin to think and act the way Jesus did. Since we're not living in perfection, never-failing love within the human heart is not possible, but seeking His heart makes *everything* possible.

The Heart Thinks

Another aspect of love, like I mentioned earlier, is that love is a choice. In order to make a decision about something, we're required to think about it first. **For as he thinketh in his heart, so is he**: *Eat and drink, saith he to thee; but his heart is not with thee* [Proverbs 23:7 KJV]. The heart actually thinks and makes decisions. One of the many amazing truths about Jesus is that He chooses, through His heart, to love us unconditionally. Knowing that Jesus chooses daily to love us unconditionally when He has the choice to stop loving us at any time boggles my mind, but not my heart.

Following your heart when it's connected to God's is wise because His heart always makes sound decisions. On the other hand, following your heart when it's disconnected from God's is unwise because the heart of man is deceitful. One of the reasons a lot of people are brokenhearted is because of the latter of the two. Many people don't believe in God's supernatural power because they're trying to figure it out with their heads and not their hearts. The problem with a broken heart is that it cannot think properly due to the pain. Some of the pain has been passed down by former ancestors through a generational curse which I talked about in the previous chapter. People who don't believe in the current activity of God's divine power may not feel brokenhearted, but that's because the curse of the broken heart didn't originate in their current generation. When the curse of the broken heart is passed onto the next generation, the inheritors don't know they've been cursed because in the eyes of the dispirited, brokenness is normal.

Operating in Brokenness

If you break your leg and go to the doctor, it will heal properly. If you break your leg and let it heal on its own, it will heal incorrectly. In both of these scenarios the leg heals, but not in the same way. The leg that heals through professional treatment will never give you any more problems, but the leg that heals on its own will give you sharp pains that come and go for the rest of your life. The sharp pains I'm talking about are: anger, resentment, bitterness, offensiveness, depression, fear, and so forth. Unfortunately, everyone experiences some of these negative emotions from time to time, but those of us who are experiencing them all the time are suffering from a leg that never properly healed. If someone has hurt you emotionally and it still hurts to think about it, you're likely operating in brokenness because of it.

When I was in fifth grade, I was walking out of the lunchroom when I overheard my teacher from around the corner say, "My students are so stupid." From that day forward, I struggled with low self-esteem up until my adult years. There's a saying I heard from a TV show that goes, "Sticks and stones may break your bones, but words will kill you." Words can sometimes have more of a negative effect on a person than physical pain itself. Today of course, I have already forgiven my teacher for what she said because I know she was operating out of brokenness. Regarding this subject, Pastor Bill Johnson used the analogy of a physical wound to describe what happens when we are healed through Christ. He said [paraphrased], "When a wound heals properly through Christ, it becomes a scar. As a scar, the memory is still there, but it is no longer painful."

A person who operates in brokenness is punishing people for the wrong things others have done to them. A very good example of operating in brokenness is what happened during the Age of Enlightenment. Because the supernatural realm isn't something that can be reasoned, it was rejected in America during that time period. Since churches around the country were forced to stop teaching and believing in the miracles of God, their hearts were broken because their freedom was violated. Generations and generations after the Age of Enlightenment ended, churches that didn't believe in the supernatural no longer knew why. They forgot about the broken hearts of their ancestors who had their freedom violated during the Age of Reason. Today, many churches don't believe in the supernatural because that's what they've been taught to believe by their previous generation. If we were to go back in time to their previous generation, they would tell us that they also didn't believe because they were convinced by their former ancestors to be skeptical.

What ends up happening is that the curse of the broken heart goes unnoticed. Operating out of a broken heart doesn't only happen with Christians, but with non-believers as well. For example, if you were abused as a child and you never healed from that negative experience, you will never truly trust anyone. Psalm 147:3 says, *He heals the brokenhearted and binds up their wounds*. There are many ways that God chooses to bind the wounds of those that are broken.

Binding Your Wounds

One of the ways the Lord heals us is through water baptism. The baptism of water is a symbol of our death and resurrection with Christ. Water baptism is not required to be a Christian, but something happens in the Spirit when there is a physical act of obedience. When we are baptized with water, it means we are dying to our past troubles and being resurrected into the righteousness of Christ. *We were therefore buried with him through baptism into death in order that, just as Christ was raised from the dead through the glory of the Father, we may too live a new life* [Romans 6:4]. The human brain is trained to believe something when the body's natural senses go through an experience. When a person's brain perceives that he/she has been physically baptized into Christ, it automatically becomes aware that there needs to be a change in that person's lifestyle. Baptism by water is a symbolic, physical manifestation of our death and resurrection with Christ; water baptism creates a bridge between the brain's natural ability to receive truth by demonstration and Jesus' supernatural ability to give it.

The Power of His Fire

Another way the Lord heals us is by His consuming fire. John answered them all, "I baptize you with water. But one who is more powerful than I will come, the straps of whose sandals I am not worthy to untie. He will baptize you with the Holy Spirit and fire [Luke 3:16]." The purpose of fire baptism is to destroy anything in our hearts that is not of God. This type of baptism leads us to repentance by giving us God's eyes to see our hearts the same way He does. Fire baptism is different from water baptism because when His fire cleanses us from our iniquities, all Heaven breaks loose. Water baptism helps us to fully grasp what Jesus already did so that when we're baptized by fire, we will demonstrate to the world what He is still doing. When Heaven breaks loose, what's normal up there becomes normal down here. Fire baptism spiritually burns negative emotions and fills our empty hearts with the fullness of His Spirit. While baptism by fire does supernaturally delete negative emotions, it doesn't erase the memories. I have heard of many people who were baptized by fire and it transformed their lives for a season, but shortly afterward they fell back into the same brokenness they had before their encounter with the Holy Spirit. The reason the transformation didn't last is because they were not renewing their minds daily as Romans 12:2 says.

In the broken leg analogy, I mentioned earlier, even if you were to receive professional treatment for your leg, running the day after you get out of the hospital will eventually put your leg back in the same condition it was in prior to your treatment. It is possible to heal from a broken heart rather quickly, but it is up to us to continue the healing process by the renewing of our minds. God's Holy fire also has the power to transform us by reading His word. Jeremiah 23:29 says, *"Is not my word like fire,"* declares the Lord, *"and like a hammer that breaks a rock into pieces?"* His fire doesn't destroy our hearts, it destroys our brokenness. Sometimes His refining process can be painful. But with that thought in mind, God doesn't refine our hearts with fire because He wants us to fail, He does it because the fire strengthens our ability to succeed. A perfect example of what I'm *not* trying to say is that God gives us diseases to make us stronger. God gives you the strength to stand up during your sickness and persevere through the pain to start walking again. Every painful step you take crushes the devil's plans. Since the devil didn't expect you to get back up from your sickness, he has no other option but to be defeated by your feet. It's usually not okay to walk all over someone, but when that someone is the devil you can make an exception.

Two verses that explain His refining process are in Zechariah 13:8–9 which says, "In the whole land," declares the Lord, "two-thirds will be struck down and perish; yet one-third will be left in it. This third I will put into the fire; I will refine them like silver and test them like gold. They will call on my name and I will answer them; I will say, 'They are my people,' and they will say, 'The Lord is our God.'" God doesn't put us into His holy fire without an explanation. When we call on Him, He answers.

The heart, as I mentioned earlier, thinks. Not only does the heart think, the heart also has the ability to see into His supernatural realm. *I pray that the eyes of your heart may be enlightened in order that you may know the hope to which he has called you, the riches of his glorious inheritance in his holy people, and his incomparably great power for us who believe. That power is the same as the mighty strength he exerted when he raised Christ from the dead and seated him at his right hand in the heavenly realms, far above all rule and authority, power and dominion, and every name that is invoked, not only in the present age but also in the one to come* [Ephesians 1:18–

21]. When we learn to enlighten our hearts instead of our heads, we will believe in His incomparably great power. Choosing to believe in His power with your Spirit instead of your head doesn't make it a hard decision, but a heart decision. With our heart's eyes open, as this verse describes, we see that God's power that raised Christ from the dead during Paul's time is the same power that has continued into our present reality! If we are not seeing into the supernatural, it's because our hearts are wide shut instead of wide open.

Now that we know that a broken heart cannot see into the supernatural [God's obviously], we need to learn how to open the eyes of our hearts to it. **His eyes [Jesus]** *are like blazing fire, and on his head are many crowns. He has a name written on him that no one knows but he himself* [Revelation 19:12]. Opening our heart's eyes to His power is as easy as praying for it [Ephesians 1:18]. As soon as we open the eyes of our hearts and gaze into the eyes of Jesus, our disbelief burns to ashes by His flames of love.

Even if you're skeptical of love, Jesus still loves you. He is a gentleman who will wait for you. He won't beat you up if you're believing horrible things about yourself. He loves you even if you don't yet love yourself. He knows every tear you've cried, and He's caught every single drop. He's waiting for the day that you will trust Him so that He can shower you with blessings from your own tears; none of them have gone to waste. Your sorrow hasn't been in vain. He will heal you if you'll simply trust Him.

Once you have has been completely restored by the divine power of Christ, the eyes of your heart become enlightened to many things; one of these things is the world of angels. The Bible talks a lot about angels and explains their importance in our lives. Angels of the Lord are given assignments to protect each one of us from calamity. Many of us believe in angels but don't know much about them. It's time for us to develop a better understanding of angels and why God created them.

Chapter Thirteen
The Angelic Realm

The Purpose of Angels

M any people believe that we have one guardian angel, but I believe each person has several. Angels are helpers of God. One of the ways they help God is by delivering messages to us from the Lord. We must not underestimate the importance of angels; after all, it was an angel of the Lord that told the virgin Mary she would give birth to the Savior of the world. That's a pretty important message right there. The job description for angels is to worship God and deliver messages from the Lord that point to Him alone. As I mentioned in Chapter Five, angels have a freewill and some of them have been fired by God for not doing their jobs.

Unemployed angels, also known as fallen angels, no longer care about what God says; therefore, they do and say whatever they please even if it hurts people. Many false religions have been founded because someone heard from an angel that wasn't of God. Galatians 1:8 says, *But even if we or an angel from heaven should preach a gospel other than the one we preached to you, let them be under Gods curse!* When Paul said, "An angel from Heaven," he was talking about fallen angels that originated from Heaven prior to them being cast out, not angels that still abide there. If we research the history of when the Bible was originally written, we will find out that it was completed long before many other well-known religions today even existed. What I'm trying to say is that many religions have started because an angel spoke to someone and gave him/her a message. The fact that an angel would speak to a person with a new "message of truth" that contradicts the Bible *after* it was written sounds a little fishy to me. God has given believers discernment to determine which angels are of God and which ones are not. When the angel speaking to us is of God however, the message not only aligns with His will, but it also encourages us and increases our faith in the Lord.

During the short time after Jesus' death, His disciples lost faith in the Lord. Even though Jesus told them that He would rise again in three days, they stopped believing because of the fact that He was dead. Jesus said that He is the way, the truth, and the life, and we need to make sure we are aligning our thinking with His truth instead of the discouraging facts around us. God's truth *always* supersedes life's facts. Getting back to the story; early one morning Mary Magdalene and some others bought spices and decided to anoint the body of Jesus, but when they arrived at His tomb, they realized the stone had been rolled away. Now there are three verses in the Bible that explain the same event regarding Mary Magdalene and the others entering Jesus' tomb, but they all seem to contradict one another. Let's take a look at these verses and I will explain why I believe the contradiction is not what it seems.

As they entered the tomb, they saw a young man dressed in a white robe sitting on the right side, and they were alarmed. Mark 16:5

They found the stone rolled away from the tomb, but when they entered, they did not find the body of the Lord Jesus. While they were wondering about this, suddenly two men in clothes that gleamed like lightning stood beside them. Luke 24:2–4

Now Mary stood outside the tomb crying. As she wept, she bent over to look into the tomb and saw two angels in white, seated where

Jesus' body had been, one at the head and the other at the foot. John 20:11–12

In these three verses, Mary Magdalene, Mary the mother of James, and Salome saw angels at Jesus' tomb, but each verse says something different. Since we don't know how many of them were actually there and who really saw what, I will only focus on Mary Magdalene since she is in all three versions of the same story. In Mark, Mary Magdalene saw one angel sitting; in Luke, she saw two angels standing, and in John, she saw two angels sitting. I personally believe that Mary Magdalene saw several angels there that day. The only verse I want to isolate is the verse in John when Mary saw two angels sitting. She was the only person out of everyone with her who noticed there were two angels sitting--one at the head and the other at the foot of where Jesus' body would have been. I believe that for some reason which we don't know, Mary Magdalene was given a greater ability to see into the spirit world to receive the good news of Christ's resurrection. The reason I mention all of this is to say that we don't all have the ability to see into the spirit world the same way. It is important for us to recognize when God is speaking to us through His angels. In Hebrews 1:14, it says that angels are ministering spirits. The meaning of the word "minister" according to the web is: to care for someone's needs or to help. The original Latin definition for the word means: "less" or "servant." What I am trying to get at, is that angels are not just servants of God, but servants of man. Angels wait in anticipation to accomplish the assignments we give to them knowing that God has revealed mysteries to us that they cannot fathom. 1 Peter 1:10–12 says,

Concerning this salvation, the prophets, who spoke of the grace that was to come to you, searched intently and with the greatest care, trying to find out the time and circumstances to which the Spirit of Christ in them was pointing when he predicted the sufferings of the Messiah and the glories that would follow. It was revealed to them that they were not serving themselves but you, when they spoke of the things that have now been told you by those who have preached the gospel to you by the Holy Spirit sent from heaven. **Even angels long to look into these things.**

I am going to better explain what this verse means. The prophets of the Old Testament prophesied the coming of Jesus Christ, His death and resurrection, and His grace for mankind that would follow. The Old Testament prophets realized they were serving us by telling us about the grace of God through Christ. How they were serving us today without ever knowing us is such a mystery that even the angels desire to look into it. The angels are mesmerized by the amount of spiritual authority God has given to us as followers of Christ. Next, I am going to share a vision the Lord showed me once during worship. This vision will explain both why angels long to look into our lifestyles as Christians, and how God uses them to help us in our ministry to save this world.

The Lighthouse Vision

One night during worship, I had a vision of an ocean as wide as the eyes could see. In the middle of the ocean was a narrow white path brighter than the sun. Straight ahead of the narrow path was a small white lighthouse titled, "The Holy House of God." Then, I saw something black. It was an evil presence darker than pitch black, and it was blocking the path to the lighthouse. The black evil presence covered the lighthouse in an attempt to stop people from seeing God's fortress. Then all of a sudden, there was an explosion within the lighthouse. The internal explosion didn't destroy it [the lighthouse], but it destroyed the darkness surrounding it. If you can imagine, the light inside of the house somehow penetrated through the opaque walls and it was seen externally as though the walls were transparent. The light broke free.

After that, I saw Jesus giving everyone in the world a hug simultaneously. In the vision, somehow I knew that the light house was impenetrable. I knew that it was rooted all the way to the bottom of the ocean where I saw it attached to a solid rock-like foundation. As we [me and apparently everyone else who wanted to come to this place for safety and rest] made our way from the narrow path into this lighthouse, we noticed that the inside of it was massive; it was the size of a football field, and that was only one room. **There were angels playing harps to the left and to the right on both sides of us, and we all [everyone who followed me along with the angels] worshipped the Lord as we saw Jesus sitting on His throne ahead of us.** As we continued walking toward Jesus, the same dark presence earlier that tried to cover the lighthouse manifested itself again in front of us. The dark presence was trying to stop us from getting to Jesus. We somehow seemed unfazed by the darkness however and walked right through it. When we finally got to Jesus He said, *"Now that you have found Me, you will NEVER be lost again. I am with you everywhere you go. Even in times you think you are lost, I am still with you."*

The meaning of this vision was later interpreted to me by the Holy Spirit. The lighthouse represents Heaven, and the narrow path symbolizes the road to Heaven which is narrow [Matthew 7:14]. Many people don't see Heaven as a real place, and if they do, they don't see it as magnificent as it really is. The ocean symbolizes the troubles of this life with the end result being death. The black presence symbolizes the devil. The devil always tries to hide the truth from those seeking it because he knows that those who find the truth won't want to turn back. When the explosion took place and the light broke free, it confirmed that light always overcomes darkness [John 1:5]. Those who seek for Jesus will find Him, and any darkness that tries to get in the way becomes destroyed by God's love. Notice that Jesus was simultaneously hugging everyone, but at the same time He was seated on His throne. The reason this is possible is because He is omnipresent.

The lighthouse not only symbolizes Heaven, but it also symbolizes our rock-solid foundation in Christ. The reason I shared this vision is to explain the significance of the angels inside the lighthouse worshiping Jesus. The supernatural power of worship breaks off demonic forces as you can see from this vision. I believe that angels of the Lord assist us in destroying the powers of the demonic not only by guarding us, but by worshiping with us. There are many ways that God speaks to and heals us, and I believe that worship is one of the most beautiful ways He chooses to do so. Worship is not only praising God through music, but it's meditating on His presence. There's a reason the angels can't stop worshiping the Lord and if we knew why, we wouldn't want to stop either.

Chapter Fourteen
The Supernatural Power of Worship

Worship Binds on Earth What is Already Bound in Heaven

I am going to start this off with one of the most amazing verses in the Bible [in my opinion] regarding the power of worship. Most of you have probably heard the story of Jehoshaphat before, but for those of you who haven't, you're in for a treat. This story gives us an example of how worship not only destroys the devil's works in the spirit world, but also in the natural world. 2 Chronicles 20:20-22 says, *Early in the morning they [Jehoshaphat and his men] left for the Desert of Tekoa. As they set out, Jehoshaphat stood and said, "Listen to me, Judah and people of Jerusalem! Have faith in the Lord your God and you will be upheld; have faith in his prophets and you will be successful." After consulting the people, Jehoshaphat appointed men to sing to the Lord and to praise him for the splendor of his holiness as they went out at the head of the army, saying: "Give thanks to the Lord, for his love endures forever." As they began to sing and praise, the Lord set ambushes against the men of Ammon and Moab and Mount Seir who were invading Judah, and they were defeated.*

I can only imagine how comical this scene must have looked to the enemies. They were probably wondering what the heck was going on when they showed up for the battle and saw the men on the opposing team barefoot while singing songs and playing instruments. The enemies however underestimated the power of God through their worship. A lot of things we do as Christians look silly to those who don't understand, but when something supernatural happens, it doesn't look so silly anymore. One of the most common forms of worshiping the Lord is with music. There are some types of worship that release God's wonders, and other types that make God wonder what we're doing.

The two rules for worship are simple. First, worship with all your heart, and second, don't do anything demonic; that's it. Aside from worshiping God with a pure heart, there are no guidelines for worshiping the Lord. Many churches however believe that worship must be done a certain way. In some churches, everyone must stand up during worship and be still. No one would even think about raising their hands to the Lord because they might be frowned upon. Worshiping the Lord is an act we do with our hearts, but if our hearts are not truly in it, the Lord takes no notice of it. Isaiah 29:13 says, *The Lord says: "These people come near me with their mouth and honor me with their lips, but their hearts are far from me. Their worship of me is based on merely human rules they have been taught."* People who worship God out of ritual are not pleasing Him. The sad truth is that a lot of people grew up in churches where worship is just another tradition. If many people start looking at their watches in the middle of a worship service, something's wrong with the worship. Worshiping with music can involve singing, dancing, shouting, painting/drawing, crying, soaking, resting, and so forth.

A great man of God from the Bible who gave us an example of what worship should look like is King David. 2 Samuel 6:14-15 tells us that David danced before the Lord with shouts of joy and trumpets blasting; now *that's* worship! There are some times worship means to sing and shout to the Lord, but other times it means to sit still and focus on God's manifest presence. Either way, there should be no judgment on how it's done as long as we're praising God with our hearts. When we worship God with our hearts, His supernatural power is released.

Worship in the Secret Place

Psalm 91:1 [KJV] says, *He that dwelleth in the secret place of the most High shall abide under the shadow of the Almighty.* I believe there is something significant about worshiping God in our secret place. There is a very subtle form of worship known as soaking that is usually done in private. Soaking is a very intimate form of worship/prayer that builds a deep connection between the individual and God. We don't go into our secret place to get something from God, but to spend time with Him. I see soaking as God recharging my batteries. In public we can sometimes act as if we've got it all together, but in private is when God really provides His healing power and direction for our lives. Worshiping the Lord in our secret place builds endurance for us to go through our trials in public. Many of the answers God gives us don't come by going to a prophet, receiving a word of knowledge, or even reading the Bible. It is important to know the Bible before going into the secret place because without knowing what His instruction manual says, we won't know what God's voice sounds like. In saying that, however, *sometimes* the answers don't come from the Bible itself, but they come from God's direct revelation.

Spending time with the Lord in private rewards us in public, not that we're seeking a reward, but because that's what He said. Matthew 6:6 [KJV] says, *But thou, when thou prayest, enter into thy closet, and when thou hast shut thy door, pray to thy Father which is in secret;* **and thy Father which seeth in secret shall reward thee** *openly."* God didn't put desires in us without an intention to fulfill them. We generally don't go into the secret place to pray for our desires, but to connect with God's presence, to thank Him for everything He's done for us, and to listen to what He wants to say. When God rewards us publicly, that means His rewards are not only spiritual but tangible. When this verse says He rewards us openly, it means that other people will notice the rewards we receive as well. The reason I bring this up, is because some people will isolate themselves from the outside world to spend time with God and stay there.

You will never receive your reward if you don't eventually come out of your secret place and continue doing what God has called you to do. Though I'm emphasizing the importance of one on one time with God, I just want to say that I don't mean permanently isolating from friends and family. With that being said, I believe that Jesus' alone time that He spent with God is what fueled Him to live the extravagant lifestyle He did. One of the many ways we can worship God in our secret place is by worshiping Him with songs of deliverance.

You are my hiding place; you will protect me from trouble and surround me with songs of deliverance [Psalm 32:7]. Soaking, as I talked about earlier, is not just a form of prayer, but it also aids in deliverance which derives from worship. Deliverance is sometimes needed when a person is overwhelmed with evil thoughts. Christians cannot become demon possessed, but we can become demon oppressed. The devil cannot overcome the mind of a believer because we have the mind of Christ [1 Corinthians 2:16], but we can be tormented with demonic thoughts. Deliverance, which is a byproduct of worship, is a way to break free from demonic oppression. The supernatural power of worship not only destroys tormenting thoughts, but it also positively affects our reality. Going back to the story of Jehoshaphat: the men worshiped God at the forefront of the battle knowing that God would deliver them from their enemies. The songs of deliverance they sang unto the Lord protected them from their troubles. I feel like sometimes deliverance is a reward from God for those of us who seek Him in our secret places.

Our Rewards for Worship

The definition of worship according to the Merriam-Webster dictionary is, "To honor or reverence as a divine being or supernatural power." With that type of definition, worship can be anything. Whatever we do that honors God is considered to be worship. *Whatever you do, work at it with all your heart, as working for the Lord, not for human masters, since you know that you will receive an inheritance from the Lord as a reward* [Colossians 3:23-24]. There seems to be a theme going on throughout the Bible that talks about receiving a reward from God for honoring Him in worship. Something really important that we must realize is that worship is all about God. There is a similarity between being poor in spirit and having the heart of a worshiper; both of them bring Heaven down in a greater measure. Some of the rewards God gives us for worshiping Him are: physical/emotional healing [deliverance], financial inheritance, closer friendships, marriage partners, and the list goes on. Again, as I mentioned earlier, we don't worship God to receive rewards, but rewards are the repercussions of our worship.

One of my favorite types of rewards from God for our worship is divine healing. The healing power of sound waves has been studied by the National Institutes of Health, and many people have reported healing in their bodies because of it. Musical instruments also generate the sound waves required to induce physical healing. I find it fascinating that the National Institutes of Health is just now discovering the healing power of our God that has already been unveiled to us through the resurrection of Christ over two thousand years ago. In my own church community, I have heard many testimonies of people being healed of physical ailments during worship. We all know that headaches don't go away on their own without aspirin and/or plenty of rest, but I can personally remember one incident when I went to my church with a migraine headache and God did something amazing in me. When I went to the front for worship, the pounding in my head was so bad that I almost had to sit down, but then I started feeling the presence of God and decided to continue standing. As the music played during worship, I started to speak to God in my prayer language [tongues] and felt a tingling sensation flowing throughout my entire body.

As the sensation continued, I went into a trance-like state of mind to where I felt almost as if I was having an out of body experience. After a while I was so lost in the presence of the Lord that I forgot I had a headache, and the reason I forgot was because it was gone! Whether we worship in our secret place or in public, God rewards us for our genuine desperation for Him. Worship connects our minds to the realm of Heaven where there is no pain or sickness. Many people ask what God's will is for their lives, and Jesus answered our question when He said, *Your will [God's] be done on earth as it is in heaven.* God's will is for Earth to look like Heaven, and worship is one of the most beautiful ways to see His will come to pass in this world.

Worship, in contrast to its life changing effects on believers, has a soporific effect on atheists. Nonbelievers don't understand the supernatural power of worship, so in their minds it's considered to be a dull activity. Many Christians tend to judge nonbelievers when they are confused by what we do for God. What we should be doing is trying to grasp where they're coming from instead of arguing. Only when we stop arguing and start listening to atheists will we finally see them as Sons and Daughters of God who have not yet found their way.

Chapter Fifteen
Comprehending the Mind of a Nonbeliever

[Reading into the thoughts of an atheist from a believer's perspective]

Christianity Should Not Be Boring Nice Guys

Friends of mine who are not saved tell me that they don't want to accept Christ because then they have to try to be good and being good is boring. If being a Christian is boring, we're not doing it right. We're already doing it wrong if we're trying to do anything. The only thing we need to do is believe because being a Christian isn't about *doing*; it's about *being*. As a Christian we're not trying to be righteous, we already are. If we sin, we don't need to beat ourselves up for it because Jesus already forgave us on the cross. But with that being said, being a righteous saint means we're dead to sin and *sinner* is no longer our identity. As a saint, we're not okay with living in sin due to the Spirit's conviction. In a sense, we're not fighting to be good people but we're fighting to keep thoughts away from telling us that we're not. Because of Christ we're not *trying* to be good, we *are* good. This may sound like arrogance to insecure people, but that's how God's sons and daughters think.

The phrase "nice guy," according to the world's standards, is defined as a person who doesn't stand up for what he believes in because he wants to avoid confrontation. The nice guy wants to avoid it because the friction of the confrontation would redefine his identity. Nice guys can't take the Kingdom by force because they're afraid of confrontation, but the violently righteous can.

Nice guys don't know how to take initiative while righteous guys do. Ephesians 5:23 says, *For the husband is the head of the wife as Christ is the head of the church, his body, of which he is the Savior.* Many foolish people believe that this verse gives men an excuse to be controlling in a relationship. Control stems from fear and insecurity, but the act of taking initiative derives from one's identity in Christ. It is impossible to be a nice guy [according to the word's standards] and a follower of Christ at the same time. Jesus said in Matthew 10:22, *You will be hated by everyone because of me, but the one who stands firm to the end will be saved.* What Jesus meant when He said that is that being a Christian is not popular. It wasn't popular back then and it's even less popular now. When I decided to rededicate myself to Christ, I lost quite a few friends. Since then, however, the amount of new friendships I've made has already surpassed the amount of friends I initially lost.

The definition of a nice guy from a worldly perspective describes a person that is a pushover but being a nice guy from a Kingdom perspective means that we've graduated to pushing the devil over. The truth of the matter is that being a Christian has nothing to do with trying to be nice. We were not created by God to be good or to be bad, but to be real. Being real requires us to be at such a high level of transparency with other people, that this action in itself rends the heavens, and provides the supernatural Godly favor necessary to propel us into our true destiny.

The Poison of the Religious Spirit

One reason religion is boring is because religion is about trying to do something in order to be something; it is the spirit of repetition and performance that slanders the Gospel. Not only is religion boring, but it's exhausting. Many people believe that if they're giving ten percent of their tithes, going to church every Sunday, praying every night, reading their daily Bible verses, and being nice people in their communities, then God is proud of them. The truth is that God is proud of us simply for existing. Doing all of these things is actually boring if we don't have a relationship with God. It also doesn't help if we've never had a tangible encounter with Him. Many nonbelievers and Christians alike view going to church as a chore; it's a hard job, but somebody's gotta do it. Jesus says that a marriage between a man and a woman is a symbolization of our oneness with Christ. No one gets married because he/she is required to, but because that person chooses to. Does anyone ever say, "Great. Now I have to be fruitful and multiply because the Bible says so. Might as well get it over with." No! No one ever says that. If marriage is designed to be exciting, then our relationship with God should be exciting too. Marriage would be boring if a husband and wife spent all day sitting at a table together reading books about how great marriage is, but never had the experience for themselves. In the same way, following Christ is not a chore, it's an experience.

Another reason religion is boring is because there's no relationship with Jesus. In a natural relationship we have natural experiences, but in a supernatural relationship, we have divine encounters. If I were an unbeliever, I would not be interested in following God if He could only be explained to me but not demonstrated. In a relationship between a man and a woman, there is a dialogue. This is the same type of dialogue we should be having with God. Dialogue is the foundation of a friendship. *I no longer call you servants, because a servant does not know his master's business. Instead, I have called you friends, for everything that I learned from my Father I have made known to you* [John 15:15]. A lot of us think God is like a wall that doesn't talk back. It's quite boring to have a conversation with a wall because there's no dialogue. Many religions around the world worship god's that don't talk back. I would be a little nervous to ask a god for help if that god was always silent. When we pray to our God in Jesus name, however, He answers.

In 1 Kings Chapter eighteen, Elijah came across many Baal worshipers. Elijah was very angry with the fact that these men were former Christians who decided to worship another god because of their unbelief. To formulate a solution to this problem, Elijah decided to create a showdown between The Lord and the god of Baal. In verses 23 and 24 Elijah said, *"Get two bulls for us. Let Baal's prophets choose one for themselves, and let them cut it into pieces and put it on the wood but not set fire to it. I will prepare the other bull and put it on the wood but not set fire to it. Then you call on the name of your god, and I will call on the name of the Lord. The god who answers by fire—he is God."* Then all the people said, *"What you say is good."*

Verses 26 through 29 say, So they [the Baal worshipers] took the bull given them and prepared it. Then they called on the name of Baal from morning till noon. "Baal answer us!" they shouted. But there was no response; no one answered. And they danced around the alter they had made. At noon Elijah began to taunt them. "Shout louder!" he said. "Surely he is a god! Perhaps he is deep in thought, or busy, or traveling. Maybe he is sleeping and must be awakened." So they shouted louder and slashed themselves with swords and spears, as was their custom, until their blood flowed. Midday passed, and they continued their frantic prophesying until the time for the evening sacrifice. But there was no response, no one answered, no one paid attention. Lastly to skip ahead, verses 36 through 39 say, At the time of sacrifice, the prophet Elijah stepped forward and prayed: "Lord the God of Abraham, Isaac and Israel, let it be known today that you are God in Israel and that I am your servant and have done all these things at your command. Answer me, Lord, answer me, so these people will know that you, Lord, are God, and that you are turning their hearts back again."

Then the fire of the Lord fell and burned up the sacrifice, the wood, the stones and the soil, and also licked up the water in the trench. When all the people saw this, they fell prostrate and cried, "The Lord—he is God! The Lord-- -he is God!" A God that answers prayers with fire from Heaven is not a boring God. You cannot have a relationship with a wall: Well I guess you could, but it wouldn't be a healthy one. You can however develop a relationship with Jesus. The dialogue exchanged within healthy relationships produces joy for both individuals. Unlike happiness, joy is a spiritual state, not an emotional state. When we are filled with the joy of the Lord, loving on atheists comes naturally.

Treasure Hunts: Loving on Nonbelievers

One day on a beautiful Friday afternoon, some friends and I went out to the streets to ask the Lord to reveal the hidden treasure inside of the hearts of unsuspecting strangers. We decided on this particular day to go to a park, split up into smaller groups, and then ask the Holy Spirit to reveal to us who to share His love with. In my group of three, we'd only been walking a short time until the Holy Spirit told me to talk to a homosexual couple sitting together at a nearby table. As we approached the couple, everyone in my group started to feel uncomfortable, including myself. But knowing that I am in charge of my feelings, I told my emotions to bow down to Jesus. After inaudibly saying that to myself, my feeling of being uncomfortable dissipated. When we reached their table, I started a conversation with them. "Hey guys, how's it goin?" I said. "Were doing okay" they replied nervously. "Today is a beautiful day; this weather is just amazing isn't it?" I said. "It really is, I love this weather!" one of them answered enthusiastically. Then I said, "Well I just wanted to let you guys know that when I was walking past this area, the Lord told me to share something with you guys." At this point we could tell that they were starting to feel very uncomfortable.

Next, I said "I just want to let you guys know that the Lord is proud of both of you. He just loves you both so much, and I'm hearing that He's proud of your hard work. I keep seeing a picture of a construction worker, and I feel very strongly that you're both working very hard and saving your money for something. The Lord says your blessing is coming." One of the guys was speechless but the other guy smiled, looked at his partner, then said, "We don't work in construction, but there is definitely something we are both currently working really hard and saving our money for." After the mood had lightened, my friends started sharing with the men what God had revealed to them as well. As our conversation came to a conclusion, I gave them my name, shook their hands and said, "Well it was nice to meet you guys, you guys are amazing, and God has some big plans for you both!" In the beginning of the conversation the men felt as if they were going to be judged, but at the end of it they felt loved. If we as Christians cannot learn to love and honor people we don't agree with, God's transforming love will never make it outside of the church walls. His perfect love breaks down those walls which enables us to transform lives where it matters the most, according to His agenda and not our own.

On another treasure hunt, my friend Rebecca and I walked past a blonde middle-aged woman sitting down on a bench. Rebecca is a very intelligent woman gifted with an ability to talk to a complete stranger without having that person feel uncomfortable. Upon spotting the woman on the bench, Rebecca boldly walked over to her and started a conversation. After they started talking, I made my way over to the bench, introduced myself, and sat down next to both of them. Rebecca and the woman talked for a few minutes before I started inaudibly hearing the word "school." As soon as the Holy Spirit revealed that to me, I said to the middle-aged woman, "Hello! I just wanted to let you know that as soon as I sat down here, I started getting a strong feeling that you're either in school or you're thinking about going back to school. I don't know exactly which one it is, but 'school' is what I'm hearing for you. I feel like the Lord will guide you in the right direction with that, and He is very proud of you that you're doing what you're called to do."

The woman stared at me for a couple of seconds as though she had seen a ghost. She then replied, "You're extremely bold to come up to me as a complete stranger and to say something like that, so I applaud you for your boldness." I smiled then said, "Are you doing anything right now with school?" The middle-aged woman answered, "I am actually a psychology teacher at a local community college." Excited, I replied "Really? That's amazing! God is so proud of you that you're doing what He has called you to do! He has even greater and more amazing things in the future planned for you!" The middle-aged woman didn't know who we were or how we knew those things about her, but she knew that she encountered God's love that day in a way that she probably never had before. 1 Corinthians 14:24-25 says, *But if an unbeliever or an inquirer comes in while everyone is prophesying, they are convicted of sin and are brought under judgment by all, as the secrets of their hearts are laid bare. So they will fall down and worship God, exclaiming, "God is really among you!"*

Treasure hunts are generally designed to work with the gift of prophecy to reveal secrets inside the hearts of unbelievers. This revelation gives skeptics an indisputable encounter with God. Doctrine can be debated, but an encounter cannot. God is in the business of bringing people closer together through His love. In this last testimony, I will share an example of God bringing unbelievers closer together.

On another afternoon in the park, my friend Kelsey and I noticed a young couple sitting down on a bench. We both heard the Holy Spirit telling us to go over and bless them, so we made our way in their direction. As soon as we started walking toward them however, the young couple immediately got up and started walking away. We were both perplexed because it would have made sense for them to walk away if they had seen us and didn't want to be bothered, but they never saw us. At a certain point we decided to stop and pray. We asked the Lord, "If it's really your will for us to talk to that specific couple, give us a sign by making them turn around and walk toward us." Only a few minutes after praying that, we saw the couple walk together into a building, and then only the woman came out and started walking in our direction. As she was passing us by I said, "Hello, how is your day going?" The young woman replied, "My day is going awesome! How's yours?" Kelsey and I were pleasantly surprised to see that this young woman was very much open to a conversation. "My day is going great as well!" I said. "Hey, well my friend Kelsey and I would like to give you and the man you were with some words of encouragement. We felt the Lord telling us some amazing things about you-- mind if we share?"

The young woman chuckled as she replied, "Well I don't really believe in God." I responded, "You don't need to believe in God to be encouraged right?" She smiled again as she replied, "That's right, sure go ahead why not!" The first word I started hearing when I was looking at her was "family." I said to the woman, "I feel like family is really important to you. I hear that the Lord is bringing both your family and your boyfriend's family closer together. I keep seeing a picture of a dinner table and I see both of your families sitting together and I see unity there." After sharing the dinner table vision, the woman's eyes opened wide. Then I said, "Does any of that speak to you right now in your life; in what way does that encourage you?" The woman paused for a few seconds while smiling, then said, "Well I'm actually visiting California from out of state to connect with my boyfriend's family. I don't believe in God, but that's pretty crazy dude!" My friend Kelsey also received a word from the Lord for the couple and she shared with the woman that their love is pure. Pure love is also known as perfect love which Kelsey was prophetically declaring over the couple's relationship. Kelsey also shared with the woman that they were an example to other couples of what real love should look like. The woman was deeply touched by these words and thanked us for the affirmations. Sometimes encouragement is all it takes to draw someone's heart closer to the Lord.

Most nonbelievers don't believe in God's divine power because it doesn't make sense, and arguing with people we don't agree with is not the heart of God. All we can do is love nonbelievers by giving them a taste of what the normally supernatural Christian lifestyle looks like. It's not the persuasion of man that transforms lives, but it's the power of the Gospel. Sometimes we're afraid to step outside of religion's box and explore God's divine realm because we don't know what to expect, but that's the point of faith. If we really believe that God is all powerful, then we should be stepping into what He's called us to do with confidence, so we can transform this world. The Gifts of the Spirit are still alive and active in the world today, and it's our job to make sure that we pass on the miraculous wonders of God to the next generation; only then will we fathom the mysteries of God that are in part as though they were fully known. In Psalms chapter seventy-one verse eighteen it says, *Even when I am old and gray, do not forsake me, my God, till I declare your power to the next generation, your mighty acts to all who are to come.*

If you've never had the opportunity to accept Jesus Christ into your heart, I would like to give you a chance to encounter love like you never have before. If you're ready, simply pray this prayer, "Jesus, I accept You into my heart as my Lord and Savior. Thank You for dying for my sins and saving me by Your grace. I trust You with my life and will follow You from this point on. I am ready for You to show me the true meaning of life in abundance." If you genuinely prayed that prayer just now, welcome to the family! I would strongly suggest to get connected with a local church that believes in a relationship with Jesus and the Gifts of the Spirit; the denomination doesn't matter. God has a special plan for your life unlike He has for anyone else, and this is only the beginning of your journey.

Ernesto Aragon is available for speaking engagements and public appearances. For more information, visit:

https://www.ernestoaragon.com/ or

contact us at

earagon.contact@gmail.com

www.ingramcontent.com/pod-product-compliance
Lightning Source LLC
Chambersburg PA
CBHW060155050426
42446CB00013B/2840